Praise for the previous e

" Kaye and Cousteau have given us a call to action. "
—*Laurie David, producer and author of* The Down-to-Earth Guide to Global Warming

" A mini treasure trove of information. "
—*Midwest Book Review: Children's Bookwatch*

" Help[s] students navigate the potentially complex and overwhelming task of making a change in their world. "
—**Professionally Speaking,** *the magazine of the Ontario College of Teachers*

" If we truly want to save and protect our water planet for future generations, then we must empower today's youth with the knowledge, technology, and tools to become tomorrow's change agents. *Going Blue* offers young people an easy-to-read guidebook that energizes and empowers an entire generation to take part in sustainable activities that will benefit and ultimately save our environment. "
—*Lori McFarling, CMO, Discovery Education*

" Jacques Cousteau would be proud of *Going Blue.* His grandson, Philippe, is taking up his challenge, and is bringing a new generation with him. Philippe and Cathryn are helping to form tomorrow's leaders and build a better future for us all. "
—*Daniel J. Basta, director, NOAA's Office of National Marine Sanctuaries*

" Following in his grandfather's footsteps, Philippe Cousteau leads a modern, passionate, and inspiring call to action to protect the planet's most precious resource—water. With *Going Blue,* he and Cathryn Berger Kaye have developed a motivational and active guide that helps young readers understand the fragility and importance of our oceans and waterways. It will inspire all to live differently. "
—*Laura Michalchyshyn, president and general manager of Planet Green, Discovery Health, and FitTV*

SECOND EDITION

GOING BLUE

SECOND EDITION

a TEEN GUIDE to SAVING EARTH'S OCEAN, LAKES, RIVERS & WETLANDS

by **Cathryn Berger Kaye, M.A.,**
with **Philippe Cousteau**
& **EarthEcho International**

free spirit
PUBLISHING®

Library of Congress Cataloging-in-Publication Data
Names: Kaye, Cathryn Berger, author. | Cousteau, Philippe, author. | EarthEcho International, author.
Title: Going blue : a teen guide to saving Earth's ocean, lakes, rivers & wetlands / by Cathryn Berger Kaye, M.A.,
 with Philippe Cousteau and EarthEcho International.
Description: 2nd edition. | Minneapolis, MN : Free Spirit Publishing, an imprint of Teacher Created
 Materials, [2023] | Includes bibliographical references and index. | Audience: Ages 11+
Identifiers: LCCN 2022059283 (print) | LCCN 2022059284 (ebook) | ISBN 9781631987465 (paperback) |
 ISBN 9781631987472 (ebook) | ISBN 9781631987489 (epub)
Subjects: LCSH: Marine ecology. | Marine pollution--Prevention. | Environmentalism.
Classification: LCC QH541.5.S3 K4 2023 (print) | LCC QH541.5.S3 (ebook) | DDC 577.7--dc23/
 eng/20230508
LC record available at https://lccn.loc.gov/2022059283
LC ebook record available at https://lccn.loc.gov/2022059284

Some project descriptions in this book are attributed to specific schools or youth groups and identified by city, state, or region. All efforts have been made to ensure correct attribution. Some of the names of young people quoted throughout the book have been changed to protect their privacy.

Text on pages 91–93 is adapted from the article "Our Blue Planet: Ocean Exploration" by Charles H. McLaughlin Jr. Technology and Children. December 1, 2005. Copyright © 2009 *International Technology Education Association*. Used with permission.

EarthEcho International and its works or products are not affiliated with, nor in any way in support of, The Cousteau Society or any of its works or trademarks.

Edited by Meg Bratsch and Cassie Sitzman
Cover and interior design by Tasha Kenyon

Printed in China

Free Spirit Publishing
An imprint of Teacher Created Materials
9850 51st Avenue North, Suite 100
Minneapolis, MN 55442
(612) 338-2068
help4kids@freespirit.com
freespirit.com

FSC
www.fsc.org
MIX
Paper | Supporting
responsible forestry
FSC® C144853

Dedication

From Cathryn: "To all the young people who transform ideas into saving this water planet. And to my father, James David Berger, who first introduced me to our ocean."

From Philippe: "To my mother, who inspired me to dedicate my life to making this world a better place. And to my daughters, Vivienne and Colette, you are why I do this work, so that we may build a better world for the next generation."

Acknowledgments

This book grew through the contributions of many. Our appreciation goes to all who gave their time, stories, and words to fill these pages. With special gratitude to:

- EarthEcho International—Mia DeMezza, Kyra Kristof, and Nicole Ross—for the collaboration, knowledge, and joy you brought to this endeavor. And Stacey Rafalowski and Sean Russell for their work on this second edition.

- Free Spirit Publishing, especially Judy Galbraith for her excitement and Meg Bratsch and Cassie Sitzman for their editing skills.

- Jane Goodall's Roots & Shoots and Youth Service America for assistance with international service stories.

- George Buckley and his students at the Sustainability and Environmental Management Program, Harvard University Extension School, for their research contributions.

- Lance Morgan at Marine Conservation Biology Institute for his thorough scientific review.

- Sachiko Cooper DaSilva, Nate Ivy, Rebecca Jim, Dave Makepeace, Nan Peterson, Jon Schmidt, Adelaide Schwartz, Yvonne Whittaker, and Shei Ascencio for great examples.

- Our "movers & shakers"—for living the courage of your convictions.

- Writers Carlyn Tani for permission to excerpt her article "Mokule'ia Campers Help Preserve Ka'ena Point" and Charles McLaughlin for permission to excerpt his article "Our Blue Planet: Ocean Exploration."

From Cathryn: "I would like to thank my husband Barry for his patience with my late writing hours and my daughters Devora and Ariel—all of whom give me encouragement and love that inspires me daily."

Contents

What Teens Think About Saving Earth's Ocean, Lakes, Rivers & Wetlands

"People see the awesome power of the ocean and think it is indestructible. I believe that ocean life needs to be protected, and since oceans are all connected, our efforts have to be global to be successful."—Ian, age 16

"For me, the ocean was all about going to the beach . . . until I found out about that mass of plastic floating in the Pacific. Where my trash goes matters. I can do something about this."—Rhea, age 15

"We need to care about our environment now to help us survive on Earth. We need the oxygen from trees, the clean water, and the healthy air that we get from taking care of what we have."—Evan, age 14

"If we use up all our natural resources, there will be no more and then the world will be in chaos. To start, kids can pick up garbage by the water and make signs and banners to warn people about what will happen if they throw garbage away carelessly."—Nabil, age 14

"Think of all the things that live in our water—the animals, the plants, the bacteria, the bugs. They are all living creatures like us, so they deserve to live just as much as we do. Imagine you lived in the water and one day a giant dumped a bunch of oil in it, and everything around you dies, and then finally you die too. See what I'm talking about?"—Maddie, age 13

"The work we do today is important for future generations. We may not see much effect in our lifetime, but we know our children will."
—Kiddest, age 17

A Call to Action from Philippe Cousteau

Philippe Cousteau is the founder of EarthEcho International, the leading nonprofit organization dedicated to building a global youth movement to restore and protect our ocean planet. He is the grandson of the legendary ocean explorer Jacques Cousteau and the son of Philippe Cousteau Sr. In this interview he explains why now is the time—more than ever—to become an environmental champion.

My grandfather's first adventures into the world at large were considerably different than the ones we embark on today. He was one of the first people to explore the ocean—his was a true journey of discovery. Few, if any, had seen the wonders of the deep captured on film. Jacques Cousteau and his crew were the first to capture those images and share them with the wider world. Imagine all the creatures we have grown up with and take for granted—from coral reefs to polar bears, Nemo the clownfish, and even SpongeBob SquarePants. All were total mysteries to the world.

My father, Philippe Cousteau Sr., who joined my grandfather on his expeditions and in his films, passed away in an airplane accident six months before I was born. Growing up with tales of their adventures, I heard stories of how they took their first underwater breaths and descended to the spectacular reefs of the Mediterranean and the Red Sea in the 1940s and 1950s. But I was also told of their devastation at seeing what happened to those very same reefs, now mere shadows of what they once were, due to climate change and pollution. Indeed, I spent many hours of my own youth diving off the coast of France and I can no longer stand to go back. I find the desolate underwater landscape so terrible. It can break your heart when you see the beauty captured by my grandfather and father on film and know that today that beauty is virtually gone.

As part of the third Cousteau generation, I recognize that while my grandfather's generation was focused on exploration, and my father's

"My role is to help build a generation of participation in restoring our ocean and waterways."

on conservation, my role is to help build a generation of participation in restoring our ocean and waterways. Of course, I am proud to have the Cousteau name. But I'm not a Cousteau only because of my name. The Cousteau spirit of conservation and care for the environment was taught to me. It lives on through me because of my actions, not my birth certificate. I know that what I do is what matters, and thus the legacy I carry is one that we can all be part of through our actions.

Daily, I consider the choices I make and the influence I can have by sharing information and ideas with others. Of the many concerns facing our environment, the excessive output of carbon into the atmosphere is, without question, the most troubling. Carbon is the leading cause of climate change. This current global crisis is changing our oceans—the primary drivers of climate

As Earth's climate changes, the domino effects are being felt around the world. For example, extreme weather, drought, plummeting biodiversity, and a continued dependence on fossil fuels are causing many of the defining conflicts of the twenty-first century and are already leading to mass migration of people. All of those are being driven by the world's changing weather patterns, which are brought about by changing currents and rising ocean temperatures and sea levels—all of which are caused by climate change. That is a bit of a simplification, but you get the idea: everything is connected to everything else on this planet, and the ocean is the key to it all.

But climate change isn't the only problem caused by carbon. The excessive output of carbon into the atmosphere is also responsible for another very scary problem that has nothing to do with climate change: ocean acidification. Ocean acidification occurs when the ocean absorbs excess carbon in the atmosphere. The carbon absorption causes ocean water to become more acidic. In turn, this means that ocean creatures that build shells— such as coral, shellfish, mollusks, and pteropods (small free-swimming snails that form the basis of many ocean food webs)—are unable to build shells and survive. If this continues, it could cause the collapse of many ocean ecosystems

"Everything is connected to everything else on this planet, and the ocean is the key to it all."

and have disastrous effects on the planet. Imagine: more than a billion people currently rely on fish for their primary source of protein. If fisheries collapse because the fish have no basic food source, those people would starve and many would go to war to feed themselves. That is just one example; others are just as serious.

If this seems pretty depressing, remember: *there is hope.* The key to helping these creatures survive is to give them the healthiest, safest environments in which to live. We know that nature, and particularly the ocean, has an incredible ability to renew itself if we help it along and give it a chance. For example, coral reefs in a pristine environment are much more likely to adapt to rising water temperatures than those already stressed from pollution and overfishing. That is good news, and it means that we must double our efforts to protect and restore our environment.

Some of the most effective solutions involve replacing the exploitation of natural resources with alternatives that protect our environment and have mutual benefits. For example, in Florida during the 1990s, gill net fishing (a very destructive form of fishing) was banned along the coast. Instead of putting the gill net fishers out of work, scientists devised a way for them to raise clams in baskets along the shore. This simple form of aquaculture was even more lucrative than gill net fishing and it protected the environment. In a short period of time, Florida went from being last in clam production in the United States to being first.

Other effective solutions focus on restoring important coastal and marine habitats like mangrove swamps (see page 48), since mangrove forests can absorb up to five times more carbon than terrestrial forests. Seagrass and kelp forests have similar benefits. This begs us to move beyond the idea of sustainability and embrace an ethos of restoration. We need to work in harmony with the ocean to restore important ecosystems if we hope to have any chance of stopping the climate crisis from becoming truly catastrophic.

> "We need to work in harmony with the ocean to restore important ecosystems if we hope to have any chance of stopping the climate crisis from becoming truly catastrophic."

We have an opportunity to change our world. The last fifty years have seen the greatest amount of destruction on this planet in history, and it is the next fifty years—our fifty years   that will decide its fate. This means demanding that our politicians take these problems seriously by expressing a willingness to make changes in our own lives. Ask yourself: "Do I really need a bigger house or a bigger car?" A comfortable life is what we all aspire to; that is human nature. However, a comfortable life could be defined by living in gracious and sustainable harmony with the planet. You have an exciting opportunity to consider what choices you will make and what distinct steps you will take to be part of both a local and a global solution.

You probably hear people tell you all the time that you can make a difference. But the truth is this: You already make a difference. *Everything you do makes a difference.* Every single one of your actions has consequences. What do you want to be the results of the actions you take every single day? Look around at the world you live in—this time with "supervision"—to see deeper into the impact of each choice. What can you be doing?

> "You probably hear people tell you all the time that you can make a difference. But the truth is this: *Everything you do makes a difference.* What do you want to be the results of the actions you take every single day?"

Start with simple things, like bringing reusable bags when you shop; finding an area in your community to clean up, protect, or restore; being "water smart" at every opportunity; and encouraging the adults in your life to vote for politicians who care about your future. Endless reports prove the number one reason adults change their behavior is because of the influence of their children . . . you have *power!*

I grew up sitting with my grandfather and listening to his life's stories, hearing the urgency in his voice, being inspired by the passion my own father had for working toward a better future. Their voices influenced me in becoming the person I am today. You could call it a family legacy, or just good teaching. Regardless, I am a firm believer that if we are to build the sustainable future we all dream of, we must do it together. Each of us—all of us—making a positive difference; that is a legacy we can all share.

Philippe Cousteau

What Do You Know?

1. "Water has no beginning, end, or middle."
   What does this statement mean?

2. What fraction of the earth is covered by water?

3. Which of the following does the ocean provide: oxygen, rain, food, or oil?

4. What percentage of the ocean has been explored: 5%, 25%, 50%, or 85%?

5. Which of your everyday activities affect the ocean?

Have you thought about our ocean and **waterways** lately? Perhaps you've seen headlines about polluted lakes and rivers, toxic drinking water, unequal access to clean water, droughts, waterborne illnesses, rising sea levels, or coral reef damage. These days more ocean species are considered endangered than ever, and human overfishing threatens to starve dolphins, sharks, and seabirds. In 2022, the world's ocean temperatures were the warmest ever recorded, following a three-year trend. New lakes and rivers are being added to endangered lists yearly. In many places, drought has dried up food crops and safe drinking water is difficult to find.

> The term **waterways** (as used in this book) includes all bodies of water on Earth apart from the ocean— from ground springs to streams, brooks, creeks, ponds, marshes, wetlands, lakes, rivers, canals, bays, lagoons, ice fields, and seas.

We have depended upon our waters since the dawn of life on this planet. They feed us, quench our thirst, help us travel and transport goods, provide medicine, create energy, and let us swim, surf, sail, and dream. However, these same waters are changing in ways that threaten our way of life now and for future generations. Our ocean and waterways are hurting. With increasing acidification in the ocean, glaciers melting at the poles, and trash accumulating everywhere, what we have taken for granted for too long needs to be addressed. And *fast*.

"We all have to take responsibility for the direction we are going. In our schools we need, from the earliest times, to get across the concept that we are connected to nature and that we are trying to find a space to sustain ourselves."

—Sylvia Earle, oceanographer

The good news is that we can do something. We can step in, learn about the issues that are all interconnected—just like our waterways—and create plans for action. We can talk with others; find out what is already being done in our communities, regions, and nations; and join in. We can come up with brand-new ideas to meet the water needs we see around us every day.

You've probably heard the phrase "going green," which means pitching in to help the environment—our forests, fields, land, and air. This remains essential. What this book proposes is to add another color to the mix by going *blue* and helping to conserve and protect our planet's water. What can you do to go blue?

Starting Now

However you found this book or it found you, these pages will help you discover ways to address community and global problems. Whatever you choose to do to help our ocean and waterways—whether it's organizing a water usage awareness campaign, cleaning a local creek, monitoring the water quality in a neighborhood pond, eating more locally grown food, growing seagrass in the classroom to plant in a local estuary, or lobbying your city council to install fishing line receptacles at a local beach—the time to start is *now*.

Did You Get the Right Answers?

Here are the answers to the questions on page 6:

1. Our ocean and waterways are all interconnected and flow without beginning, middle, or end.

2. A full three-fourths of the earth is covered by water, making ours truly a "water planet."

3. The ocean provides all four of these things: oxygen, rain, food, and oil.

4. Only 5 percent of the ocean has been explored by humans, which leaves plenty for you to do!

5. And every single one of your daily activities affects our ocean and waterways—from the electronics you use, to the clothes you put on, to the foods you eat. By reading on, you will find out exactly how these choices and others reach to the furthest depths of the ocean.

What's Inside?

This book is filled with curious questions, eye-opening facts, useful information, inspiring quotes, amazing photos, extraordinary stories, and plenty of examples of what teens just like you are doing to keep this planet of ours healthy. All this information is divided into five stages: *Investigation*, *Preparation*, *Action*, *Reflection*, and *Demonstration*. (Each stage is explained in detail starting on page 10.) You'll also notice four repeating sections throughout the book. The *Teens in Action* sections tell stories of real teens across the world who have made or are making significant contributions. The *Your Turn* boxes help you relate the topics discussed to your own life and give you ideas for getting involved. The *Time for Reflection* boxes ask questions that encourage you to pause, think, and look at the larger picture of what you are doing. And the *EarthEcho* boxes suggest tips for how to transform the information and ideas that you read here into simple day-to-day actions that benefit the planet.

How to Read This Book

There is no one "right" way to read this book. You might decide to plunge in and read it straight through, from beginning to end. Or you can pick and choose sections that interest you at a given time, or that relate to something you're interested in or already doing.

To help navigate whichever route you choose, each of the five stages is introduced with an example of what an actual group of teens did at that stage in their own going blue journey (see *The Story of Tar Creek, Parts #1–5,* beginning on page 18), and each ends with a box briefly summarizing its contents.

Beware that once you dive in, there may be no returning to the surface. You may realize it's time to change the tide and reclaim your water planet. You may feel compelled to join in the challenge to investigate, explore, brainstorm, plan, and get involved to improve your world. You may find yourself a changed person. You may even find yourself turning a little . . . **blue.**

Tips for Using this Book

- You are holding a written guide, but you will find other guides around you—adults you meet who know about our waters, or friends, family, and community members who are eager to help. People across the globe are getting involved every day. Ask them questions. Learn what they have to share.

- Use a journal to keep track of your thoughts and observations as you read.

- Stay informed about current news involving our ocean and waterways, including issues of climate change and global warming, as well as restoration efforts.

- Visit the many websites listed in this book to find additional information and resources.

- Involve others in your journey—friends, family, neighbors, a class, or a youth group. Learn, think, laugh, and work together to get the job done.

- Let your creativity inspire you to be an agent of change. Planet Earth needs **you.**

The Five Stages: Moving from Ideas to Action

So, how do the five stages fit into all this? Simple: these stages provide a roadmap that can guide you from where you are now to where you want to be—helping rescue our planet's water by using your knowledge, skills, interests, energy, and enthusiasm. This section introduces you to the stages and provides examples of what you can do at each.

Stage 1: Find Out—Investigate

"People can only protect what they love, but they can only love what they know."—Philippe Cousteau Sr., explorer

Your going blue journey begins the way you begin many things: you *investigate*. What do you investigate? First, you investigate the resources that you bring to helping this planet. Then, you investigate the needs in your community related to Earth's ocean and waterways.

 Create an Inventory of Your Skills and Talents Do you enjoy photography, writing, art, research, math, or science? Are you a behind-the-scenes organizer, or do you prefer being onstage with a microphone? Throughout your going blue journey, your interests and abilities can be further developed. Stretch your mind as you think of all your strengths. If you are going blue with a friend, interview each other to discover skills and talents. Ask questions. Make a list and keep it visible as you prepare, act on, demonstrate, and reflect upon your ideas. This list can be helpful at every stage of your voyage.

What Community Needs Interest You? Start a list and then discuss it with others and let your list grow. What topics are of greatest interest to people you speak with? Which ones capture the attention of just a few? What are community assets and strengths around water issues? What's going well and who is already working on solutions to pressing problems? Here's a surprise: nearly every community need you can think of will have something to do with water. As you read on, you will find out how.

Investigation Example: Water Audit

Sometimes a community need appears in the form of a question. That happened when one middle school student asked: "How much water do we use?" This led her class to the challenging task of investigating and evaluating water usage at their school and in their homes: Were they wasting water? How could they find out? What could they do about it?

The students learned to read water bills and took a walking tour of their school to identify ways to conserve water. They developed a survey for home use to record how much water each family member used per week. They compared the results with the average water use in the United States of 156 gallons per person per day. After hearing a guest speaker describe strategies for water reduction at home and conducting research, students created and distributed a family-friendly guide. *Save Water. We Need Every Drop*

Reread the previous paragraph. What skills and talents did the students put to use? What techniques did they use to investigate the community need? This will help you begin to investigate water issues in your own community.

Stage 2: Dive In—Prepare

"It takes as much energy to wish as it does to plan."
—Eleanor Roosevelt, former first lady of the United States, author, humanitarian

Now that you've investigated, the next stage in making a difference for water is to *prepare*. You have experience preparing all the time. You prepare for school in the morning; you prepare for a basketball game by shooting hoops. You prepare by learning lines for a play or gathering ingredients to bake cookies.

Preparation Example: Flood Readiness

Imagine that your community experiences severe flooding. The flood might be due to a storm, to problems with overdevelopment, to soil erosion, or to some other cause. After investigating the issue, you decide to find ways to help people in your community know what to do if flooding occurs again. How would you prepare to help your community be ready for a flooding disaster? Answer this question on your own first *before* reading the list below.

Now look at this list. Did you have similar ideas?

- Talk to people who work for emergency relief services, such as the Red Cross. Find out what they require for a flooding emergency. Do they need common supplies that could be collected, like blankets? What do they suggest people do to prepare for a flood?

- Speak to rescue workers, such as paramedics or firefighters. Are local maps accurate enough for them to reach the most remote homes in your community? What did they do in prior crises that was effective?

- Interview community members who were affected by past floods. What advice do they have about preparedness?

- Visit the location where people have been relocated during past floods, such as a school gymnasium or community center. What would make this place more welcoming—for adults, children, and pets—if it is needed again for this purpose?

- Read about the causes of flooding in your community and what can be done to prevent it. Educating the community about flood awareness could be part of your action plan.

- Check out local newspaper coverage of recent floods. Who in your local government has ideas and knowledge about the issue? Can you meet with this person?

Part of preparation is finding people and organizations that care about the community need you've chosen to address. Gather the contact information for these people and build a team that can help you plan. This includes brainstorming ideas and generating possibilities. Think big and wide—all this preparation and planning leads to the next stage . . .

Stage 3: Get Going—Act

"If you're walking down the right path and you're willing to keep walking, eventually you'll make progress."—US President Barack Obama

Once you have investigated your interests, skills, and community needs, and are prepared with background knowledge, you are ready to create and carry out a plan to *act*. Action typically occurs as direct **service,** indirect service, advocacy, research, or a combination of several of these approaches.

> **Service** means making a contribution and partnering with others for mutual benefit and the common good.

Direct Service:
Your service involves face-to-face interactions or close contact with people, animals, or the environment—such as rivers, lakes, the ocean, or any part of the watershed that is near you.

Indirect Service:
Your action is not seen by the people or animals who may benefit from it, but it meets a real need.

Advocacy:
What you do makes others aware of an issue and encourages them to take action to change a situation.

Research:
You gather and report on information that helps a community.

Action Example: Flood Readiness

Using the scenario of flood readiness again, here are examples of the different types of action that students have taken.

Direct Service: Students collected books, games, and toys and placed them in bins to be stored in the school gymnasium for use during flooding emergencies. They would then be able to lead activities with young children, entertain pets, and help families cope with the difficult situation.

Indirect Service: In case of flooding and evacuation, what documents must a family take with them? Students prepared large envelopes with a list of all the necessary documents—birth records, insurance papers, medical information, pet information. Families can place that paperwork inside the envelopes and take everything with them in case of an emergency evacuation.

Advocacy: A youth group learned how commercial development had caused soil erosion, leading to increased risk of flooding. They worked with local politicians to hold a town forum to discuss local concerns and advocate for zoning to protect fragile areas.

Research: Using photography, video, and podcasts, students documented the experiences and effects of flooding in their community and compiled a report for response teams and civic groups.

Four Action Strategies

What if you wanted to address toxic dumping in your local waterways? Think of an example for each of these four types of action.

Stage 4: Think Back—Reflect

"The most important thing is to actually think about what you do. To become aware and actually think about the effect of what you do on the environment and on society. That's key, and that underlies everything else."—Jane Goodall, environmentalist

What is one piece of information you have learned so far that you want to remember? What is one idea you have now that you didn't have before opening this book? When you answer these questions, you *reflect*: you look at your experience and consider what it means for you now and how you can use it in the future. Reflection takes place as you investigate and prepare, as you take action, and as you demonstrate what you have learned and accomplished. You will find reflection built into this book in the *Time for Reflection* boxes and in a series of questions in the Reflection section on pages 134–135.

Stage 5: Tell It—Demonstrate

"Not only is your story worth telling, but it can be told in words so painstakingly eloquent that it becomes a song."—Gloria Naylor, novelist and educator

In this final stage, you review what you learned, how you planned, what you did, and how you've reflected along the way. Then you tell others; you **demonstrate**. Here, you can again draw upon your interests and abilities to showcase your efforts to address water issues. How you tell your story is up to you. Will you:

- Make a mural?
- Create a website or blog?
- Post on a social media account?
- Build a display for your school, town hall, or community event?
- Produce a PowerPoint presentation?
- Perform a skit for a class or youth group?
- Record a video or podcast?
- Write an article for a school or community newspaper?
- Create a comic book or brochure showing the steps you took?

Going Blue can serve as your guide as you investigate, prepare, act, reflect, and demonstrate—all toward saving Earth's ocean and waterways. So let's get started!

STAGE 1
FIND OUT→INVESTIGATE

The first step in your journey to protect and restore water resources is to find out more about yourself and your skills and about the community you are trying to help. In this stage, you will learn about the issues and identify a water-related need that you want to address.

The Story of Tar Creek: Part 1

Miami, Oklahoma, United States

Brownish orange in color, Tar Creek stretches across the northeastern tip of Oklahoma, a region suffering from almost a century of lead and zinc mining that has left behind a mess of residue.

Starting here with Investigation (Stage 1), you will follow the story of Tar Creek. You'll learn how a group of young people investigated, planned, acted, reflected, and demonstrated to make a difference for a water issue in their community.

Imagine seeing mountains of toxic waste wherever you looked. Students in Miami, Oklahoma, lived in these surroundings, where mining waste poisoned their land, water, and air. In fact, their community was so badly polluted that it has been identified as a **Superfund site.** At the local high school, students and their counselor, Rebecca Jim, took on the challenge of educating the community about their hazardous surroundings—including Tar Creek, one of the most polluted bodies of water in the United States. They became knowledgeable advocates determined to save their community.

A **Superfund site** is identified by the Environmental Protection Agency as a place where toxic waste has been dumped and needs to be cleaned up. Nearly 1,900 Superfund sites exist across the United States. Around 21 million US Americans (or 6 percent of the US population) live within one mile of a Superfund site, and roughly 73 million (or 22 percent) live within three miles of a Superfund site.

How Did They Investigate?

The initial group of students who took on the Tar Creek challenge used various means of research to uncover the need. They documented their observations with photography and personal stories, and they mapped areas that seemed most impacted. They studied the history of mining in the area to root out the causes of the toxicity. They interviewed local ranchers and community elders to gather accounts of what they had seen and experienced over time. Based on this rich evidence, students defined a real need: community awareness to prevent exposure to Tar Creek's polluted water and other waste from mining.

The Story of Tar Creek continues on 60.

Tar Creek Superfund site photo credit: Janice Curtis

Getting Started:
Your Water, Your Community, Your World

What needs to be uncovered about water in your community? Become a detective and find out what you need to know.

Get Active in Your Research

Have you ever received an assignment to do research and headed straight to Google? That's one way to research. Another way is to do *action research*—where you still use technology, but you also get to do much more. As you investigate the water situation in your community and the larger world, consider using these four action research methods. The acronym MISO can help you remember them.

- **Media** includes books (such as the one you are reading right now), newspapers, magazines, movies, television, maps, and the internet—websites, blogs, social media, video-streaming sites, and other online sources. Think of ways you can work with different media to learn more about water-related topics.

- **Interview** typically involves a person with expertise or experience in a specific area. You will find many experts giving advice in the pages of this book. Can you think of someone you know personally whose work involves water? You might also ask around at school or in your community or search online to find a good person to talk to.

- **Survey** gathers information from a group of people. You read about students conducting a survey of water usage in their school and homes on page 11. Surveys help you obtain facts, opinions, and ideas. Who could you survey about water issues in your community—students, family members, neighbors, business owners, government officials, scientists, or teachers? How many surveys would you want to complete to get a full perspective on the issues?

- **Observation and experience** draws upon what you already know, have seen, and have done, and what you may venture out to see starting this very moment. Have a camera? Taking photos or videos of what you see around you tells a powerful story.

As you use these research methods, note which you like best. You may find you are a budding journalist who enjoys combining interviews and photos, or a statistics wizard who loves compiling survey results. Keep the MISO methods in mind whenever any kind of research is calling you.

Be a Critical Consumer

As you investigate and research the issues and facts surrounding Earth's ocean and waterways, be aware that not everything you read or hear is accurate. It is up to you to try to separate the fact from the fiction. Consider your sources of information: Are they dependable? Are they nonbiased (providing information regardless of their own interests)? Currently many opinions exist about the condition of our environment, the causes of its condition, and what should be done as a result. For example, scientific studies and research show how human industry plays a key role in global warming and climate change and how these are devastating our planet, and yet there are still detractors. Always validate your sources of information and be prepared to use this information to defend your statements and actions if needed.

You're All Wet!

A quick look at human anatomy lets us know that going waterless is not an option. We are simply *all wet*. Our brains alone are nearly three-quarters water, our lungs are a full 90 percent water, and our bodies on average consist of 70 percent water . . . just like this water planet we live on.

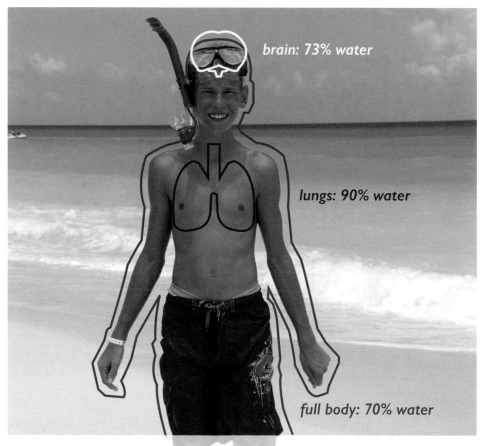

brain: 73% water

lungs: 90% water

full body: 70% water

Life Takes Water

In addition to your body, everything about you requires water. Your home is built from materials grown or produced with water. The food you eat needs water to be grown, processed, and shipped. The clothes you wear—you guessed it: water. Is there anything you use that doesn't rely on water in its production? Not much. Check out the following chart that shows how much water is used to make, process, and transport some common goods.

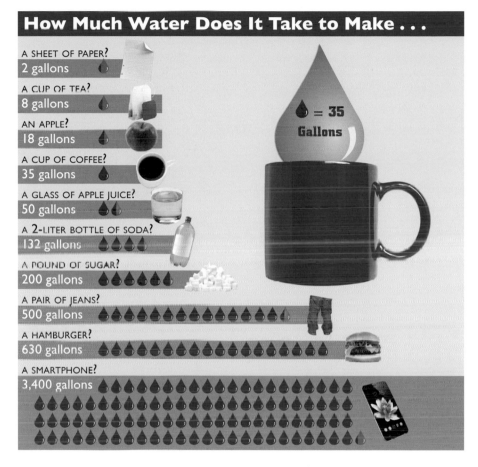

How Much Water Does It Take to Make . . .

A SHEET OF PAPER?
2 gallons

A CUP OF TEA?
8 gallons

AN APPLE?
18 gallons

A CUP OF COFFEE?
35 gallons

A GLASS OF APPLE JUICE?
50 gallons

A 2-LITER BOTTLE OF SODA?
132 gallons

A POUND OF SUGAR?
200 gallons

A PAIR OF JEANS?
500 gallons

A HAMBURGER?
630 gallons

A SMARTPHONE?
3,400 gallons

= 35 Gallons

Now you're probably wondering: *Why so much water?* Consider all that goes into producing these items. To make a hamburger, most of the 630 gallons of water go into growing grain to feed the cattle. To make your favorite pair of jeans, water is used to grow, process, and dye the cotton and keep the factory operating. Water also is used in the plant that manufactures the plastic bottle that holds your soda . . . and in the freighter that transports your Colombian-grown coffee beans to your grocery store.

What does this mean about the choices you make every day? Do your choices matter?

If you are a typical person living in the United States, you use an average of 156 gallons of water every day.

Consider that . . .

When you . . .	you use . . .
Flush a toilet	2–5 gallons per flush
Take a shower	2–5 gallons per minute
Fill a bathtub	36–50 gallons
Brush your teeth	4 gallons if the tap is running
Wash your hands	4 gallons if the tap is running

World Water Monitoring Challenge is an international education and outreach program that builds public awareness and involvement in protecting water resources around the world by engaging citizens to conduct basic monitoring of their local waterways. Visit monitorwater. org for more information.

Note that even how you *discard* your waste takes a lot of water. And this list does not even include countless other activities—such as drinking water, cooking food, washing your clothes, watering your lawn, and running a dishwasher.

YOUR TURN

How Do I Love Water? Let Me Count the Ways . . . Can you think of other ways that you use water every day? Make a list. Ask others how they use water. Challenge a friend to a see who can list the most uses for water. Combine your lists. This may lead to a water usage awareness campaign in your school or community.

TEENS IN ACTION

Valenzuela, Philippines
Make Water a Game

When students at Valenzuela City School of Mathematics and Science heard about the Global Student Innovation Challenge hosted by Xylem, Inc., they were inspired to put their great ideas into action to "Solve Water." Entrants were tasked with creating a solution to the global problem of water resource depletion through an eight-week virtual competition. The students, who called themselves team DROPEES, decided to make water conservation a game! They created the DROPEES app, which hosts young people in the Philippines to play water-related games, do real-life tasks for water protection and conservation, and support water-related organizations by donating. The app was a hit and led to team DROPEES winning third place!

La Habra, California, United States
Water Guardians

When four Sonora High School students noticed water being wasted in the school bathrooms, they wanted to see a change but had no idea just how far they would go. When they inventoried school water usage, they concluded that just by switching from regular to low-flow toilets the state of California's K–12 school system could potentially conserve 20 million gallons of water a day!

This was a huge finding, especially in a drought-plagued area like California, so the students knew they wanted to act. They developed a conservation plan for their school that resulted in a 30 percent reduction in water use and won first place in the 2015–2016 Lexus Eco Challenge. Part of that plan included poster and video campaigns at their school sharing tips on water conservation and YouTube videos encouraging other teens to conserve water. These campaigns earned the students the title of the La Habra Water Guardians.

The Water Guardians wanted to ensure the sustainability of their efforts and expand their impact, so they began working with local legislators to turn their proposal around statewide water conservation measures for schools into a bill. The teens assisted Assemblyman Phillip Chen in crafting Assembly Bill 1343, or the Go Low Water Conservation Partnerships bill, which allowed school districts to partner with their water providers to implement conservation efforts and reduce water usage in schools. Ultimately, their bill created a program where utilities offer water rebates for schools that implement water-saving measures inspired by the four La Habra Water Guardians.

You might think that once their bill passed, the Water Guardians would relax and congratulate themselves on a job well done. But the students didn't stop there. They kept going, starting water conservation clubs at both their current and former schools. Their advice for students? "Sometimes it's going to be hard and you're going to meet with a lot of challenges, but you should never give up because there's always a way. And if you really want it and work hard for it, you can accomplish anything."

Turning off the tap is the obvious way to use less water. But did you know you can instantly turn your toilet into a low-flow version? Simply fill a used plastic bottle with water and put the full bottle in the tank of your toilet. The number of ounces that the bottle holds is how much water you save every time you flush!

World Water Use

Is water usage the same everywhere in the world? Not at all. Only a small percentage of the world's population consumes the majority of its water resources. People living in the United States consume the most. The following chart shows the average daily water use in some of the world's nations.

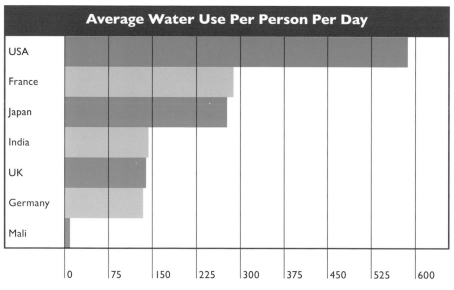

Average Water Use Per Person Per Day

Liters Note: One liter equals slightly more than four cups.

Why do you think this is the case? Unfortunately, with all the water on our water planet, there is not an endless supply for people everywhere to use, as you will read in the next section.

Water, Water Everywhere . . . or Is It?

- Seventy-one percent of Earth's surface is covered by the ocean.

- The average depth of the ocean is two-and-a-half miles.

- The average temperature of the ocean surface is 20 degrees Celsius (68 degrees Fahrenheit) and about 2 degrees Celsius (about 36 degrees Fahrenheit) at depth.

- The Pacific Ocean is the largest body of water in the world, covering 33 percent of Earth's surface.

- The Arctic Ocean is the smallest ocean basin, holding only 1 percent of Earth's seawater. This is still more than twenty-five times as much water as in all the rivers and freshwater lakes combined.

- Antarctica has as much ice as the Atlantic Ocean has water.

- The average sea level has risen between four and ten inches over the past hundred years alone.

- Ninety-seven percent of the world's water is in the ocean.

- The largest living structure on Earth is in the ocean. It is the Great Barrier Reef, which covers an area larger than Great Britain and can be seen from space.

- Three-quarters of the world's largest cities are located by the sea.

- More than 90 percent of the goods traded between countries are carried by ocean freighters.

Jane Goodall's
roots & shoots
www.rootsandshoots.org

Jane Goodall's Roots & Shoots program is a global network of young people taking action to make the world a better place. Find out more at their website rootsandshoots.org.

> "How inappropriate to call this planet
> Earth, when clearly it is planet Ocean."
> —Arthur C. Clark, author

It's a Watery World

Our planet has one big, connected ocean, yet there are many ocean basins, such as the Atlantic, Pacific, Indian, Arctic, and Southern. The ocean covers nearly three-quarters of Earth's surface, making Earth mostly water, just like our bodies.

What's more, *all* water on Earth is connected—and not just on the surface. Water evaporates from the earth's surface and falls as precipitation in the form of rain, snow, and sleet back onto the land, ocean, and waterways. It then returns to the ocean as river runoff and groundwater flow. This exchange of Earth's water in the process of evaporation and precipitation is known as the *hydrologic cycle.*

Wouldn't having endless sources of new water be fantastic? Maybe these exist in fairy tales, but not in reality. Although the ocean is large, covering the vast majority of our planet, water is finite and resources are limited.

> ❝ Today, a lot of management of natural
> resources isn't guided by science but
> by wishful thinking. ❞
> —Philippe Cousteau

Community Water Needs

Let's do the math: as shown on page 27, 97 percent of the world's water is ocean salt water. Another 2 percent is locked in ice caps and glaciers. That means 99 percent of Earth's water is unfit to drink, leaving just 1 percent freshwater for consumption by all living creatures, including plants and animals.

Most likely when you want a drink of water, you turn on a tap. But can everyone in the world do this? Are we getting "tapped out" with overuse of water in some parts of the world and extremely limited water access in others? In many areas, drought has drastically reduced access to fresh water. Climate changes have resulted in parched land and low water tables. And in many locations, water supplies are contaminated or private corporations are trying to gain ownership of public water supplies, limiting people's access.

Potable Water

Potable water is water that is drinkable—safe for human consumption. Potable water is free from pollution, harmful organisms, and impurities. In the United States, the Environmental Protection Agency (EPA), using guidelines defined by Congress in the 1974 Safe Drinking Water Act (SDWA), is responsible for setting the standards for drinking water. In addition to the EPA, each of the fifty states, plus the District of Columbia, has a governmental agency that is responsible for setting standards that meet or exceed the EPA guidelines and enforcing these drinking water standards.

> "Filthy water cannot be washed."
>
> —West African proverb

In the United States, millions of people receive high-quality potable water every day from public water supply systems via their taps. However, safe drinking water cannot be taken for granted, because this access to clean water is highly unequal. Poorer and rural communities are far more likely to have unsafe or contaminated water than wealthier or urban ones. Several things threaten public water supplies: chemicals that are improperly disposed of, animal waste, pesticides, human waste, storm water runoff, underground waste storage, and naturally occurring substances can all contaminate drinking water. Likewise, water that is not properly treated or disinfected, or that travels through a poorly maintained distribution system, may also pose a health risk.

A Thirsty World in Crisis

Internationally, the World Health Organization (WHO) is responsible for providing guidelines that can be used by all countries to define their own drinking water standards. Unfortunately, in many countries these standards are far from acceptable. For example, the WHO estimates that two billion people across the globe use a drinking water source contaminated with feces. Nearly 90 percent of all diseases in the world are caused by unsafe drinking water, inadequate sanitation, and poor hygiene. And it's estimated that around 829,000 people die each year from diarrhea from unsafe drinking water, inadequate sanitation, and poor hygiene.

A boy collects drinking water during a shortage in Delhi, India, in September 2007.
© Paul Prescott | Dreamstime.com

What can be done? Potable water needs to be treated as a limited, nonrenewable resource. While Earth's hydrologic cycle shows us that water is constantly being renewed, pollution often causes the water in our air, rain, snow, and ground springs to be contaminated. It is important we take action to:

- use water more efficiently, especially in farm irrigation methods, which currently require vast amounts of water

- conserve water in our homes, schools, and businesses

- promote the reuse of water when possible and create new methods for reclaiming wastewater

- reduce impervious surfaces (like asphalt and concrete) to allow water to flow through the soil to recharge aquifers

- limit our water consumption by buying fewer products, reusing items, or thrifting items

- make choices about the foods we consume and the products we purchase by understanding our water footprint (waterfootprint.org)

Do the environment (and yourself!) a favor and use a dishwasher instead of doing dishes by hand. An automatic dishwasher uses an average of six fewer gallons of hot water per cycle (or over 2,000 gallons per year) than hand washing.

Get Involved with Potable Water

As kids learn about the potable water crisis across the globe, many are compelled to action. Find out what kids have done and are doing and how you can join in the cause at these sites:

Ryan's Well Foundation (ryanswell.ca) was founded by Ryan Hreljac, who joined the clean water cause in 1998 at age six; his foundation has since taken on over five hundred projects in sixteen countries, bringing clean water and sanitation services to over 640,000 people.

Clean Water Action (cleanwateraction.org) is a US grassroots organization working to empower people to take action to protect the nation's waters, build healthy communities, and make democracy work for all of us.

Water.org (water.org) is a nonprofit organization whose founders have transformed hundreds of communities by providing access to safe water and sanitation.

Saving Water Worldwide

Efforts are being made around the world to save water on a daily basis. Here are a few notable ones:

- Many public facilities in countries around the world have installed sinks that have motion sensors to turn water on and off, preventing water waste.

- Some facilities use special toilet attachments that flush liquid and solid waste into separate tanks, enabling liquid wastewater to be filtered and reused in the toilets.

- Many offices and personal residences around the world use greywater systems that recycle gently used water from bathroom sinks, showers, tubs, and washing machines to flush toilets or water grass and other ornamental plants.

- In many cities, residents are allowed to water their lawns and gardens only on specified days and at specified times.

- In many places, public showers operate on a limited time basis and shut off automatically after the allotted number of minutes.

TEENS IN ACTION

Flint, Michigan, United States
Little Miss Flint

You've probably heard about the water crisis in Flint, Michigan. In Flint, lead from aging pipes leached into the city's water, causing many residents to become very, very sick, and causing at least twelve people to die.

In this book, you'll read about the many problems single-use plastic water bottles cause, but in a lot of places where water is unsafe to drink or not readily available, people must rely on bottled water for drinking, cooking, bathing, and other needs. Beginning in 2014, this was the case in Flint, and residents were told that it would take until 2020 for all the lead pipes to be replaced and their water to be safe again. In the meantime, the city government gave people free bottled water. However, in 2018, the governor of Michigan declared Flint's water safe to drink and ended the free water program.

Mari Copeny and other Flint residents knew the issue wasn't completely cleared up, since the pipes leading to many homes in Flint hadn't been replaced. When she was ten years old, Mari raised $25,000 to buy over 150,000 bottles of water, and she distributed them to members of her community during weekly events. In addition to fundraising, Mari started a letter-writing campaign to send messages of support to kids in Flint who were most affected by the water crisis.

In 2022, it was estimated that around 1,900 homes in Flint were still waiting for their pipes to be replaced. So Mari continues to raise awareness about the Flint crisis and other issues and unfair situations that low-income communities and communities of color face. She also

Want to know more about potable water? Visit these sites:
Safe Drinking Water Act (SDWA): epa.gov/sdwa
World Health Organization (WHO) Water, Sanitation, and Hygiene: who.int/health-topics/water-sanitation-and-hygiene-wash
Centers for Disease Control and Prevention (CDC) Drinking Water: cdc.gov/healthywater/drinking
Project WET Foundation—Water Education for Teachers: projectwet.org

partnered with a company called Hydroviv to create a water filter that can help end the need for bottled water in areas like Flint. The filters have been shipped all over the United States to people who do not have access to clean water.

Ayni, Tajikistan
Teaching Clean Water

Students from a secondary school in Tajikistan planned "Alternative Approaches to Water Supply." Their home is in the Ayni district, an isolated mountainous area physically cut off from the rest of the country for four to five months a year due to heavy snow and undevel-

Consider volunteering with organizations that help our environment like the ones listed in this book. Getting involved builds skills and experience that will prove valuable in school and beyond.

oped roads. The local economy is based on a mix of animal herding, orchard tending, and trade, and residents rely on open water sources, which often carry diseases. Ayni students conducted activities with younger children, teaching them how to boil water, use chlorine tablets to keep water clean, and wash their hands, and why all these things are necessary.

Niankorodougou, Burkina Faso
Moringa to the Rescue!

In the town of Niankorodougou, Burkina Faso, the Club du Science consists of the top two science students in each grade from the local junior high schools. The club studied gardening, and after reviewing uses for many of the area's native trees, they chose to focus on the many benefits of moringa trees. Originally from India, *Moringa oliefera* is a tree adapting remarkably well in Africa due to its low water needs and rapid growth. The leaves of the tree are a good source of vitamin A, vitamin C, potassium, calcium, and protein. Scientists claim that moringa helps prevent over three hundred illnesses.

In addition, grains taken from the branches of the tree can be used as a water treatment. Peace Corps member Adelaide Schwartz explains: "So many of the sicknesses here are waterborne. Clean water is hard to obtain. The moringa grain acts like a flocculent, which means when it is added to a bucket of water, within a few minutes a film can be scooped from the top, leaving behind clean water." With assistance from Ms. Schwartz and their teacher Mr. Some, the club members took their knowledge of moringa trees to the local health clinic and planned their course of action. They explained the benefits of the tree to clinic workers and planted ten trees for use in the surrounding community. Students continued to provide needed information through a community awareness campaign showing how moringa grains can be used to purify water. The students were proud to be able to help their families and community.

moringa tree in Etosha National Park, Namibia

Water Privatization

Water privatization is the process by which corporations (and sometimes governments) take control of public water supplies for private sale. Water is a $400 billion industry—the third largest in the world, behind electricity and oil. This includes private corporations that sell bottled water, as well as those that pump, disinfect, transport, and control access to water.

Water Is Big Business

- Bottled water costs thousands of times more than tap water to produce.

- The United States produces 40 billion plastic bottles each year, which requires about 17.6 million barrels of oil—enough to fuel about 1.5 million cars a year.

- Most US Americans pay $0.002 per gallon for unfiltered tap water. Filtering tap water with a countertop unit costs $0.25 per gallon, and filtering it with a unit under the sink only costs about $0.10 per gallon.

- Bottled water typically costs about $1 for an eight- to twelve-ounce bottle, amounting to more than $10 per gallon.

- In the United States, water privatization is typically the result of corporations using public water supplies and private wells to produce bottled water. Overseas, especially in underdeveloped countries, privatization often involves both the production of bottled water and the entire water infrastructure—the means to pump, distribute, and sell the water.

How much water can safely be privatized? A typical water bottling plant might take anywhere from 100 million to 300 million gallons a year from a public water supply. This heavy use of public water systems can threaten local water table levels, groundwater flow rates, and conditions of local bodies of water.

Also, if some people have free access to natural resources and others do not, could this cause conflicts? Absolutely. Global conflict between countries stemming from lack of available natural resources (food, water, oil, farmland) and the political and economic consequences of this lack of necessities is increasing. Already, water disputes are brewing between many countries that share freshwater reserves. Sensitive negotiations must occur quickly to determine how these nations will share rivers, reservoirs, and groundwater.

women collecting water from a public pipe during a water rationing period in Bhaktapur, Nepal, December 2009

© Shariff Che' Lah | Dreamstime.com

time for
REFLECTION

"Hey, that water is mine!" What do you think of people owning what previously has been public water? Should we privatize our natural resources and pay for their use? Consider the pros and cons. Who might benefit? Who might lose out?

Bottled Water

People in the United States buy an estimated 50 billion single-serving bottles of water a year—up from 3.3 billion in 1997. In the United States, more than 2.7 million tons of plastic are used each year to make water bottles. Less than 20 percent of these plastic bottles are recycled. Does using all this plastic and drinking the water inside make a difference?

In most cases, tap water actually follows higher purity standards than bottled water.

In 2006, more than 17 million barrels of oil were used to manufacture plastic water bottles. This generated more than 2.5 million tons of carbon dioxide.

While some are recycled, a whopping nine out of ten water bottles end up as garbage or litter. In the United States, cities pay around $70 million every year in costs related to trash cleanup and landfills.

The process of manufacturing a plastic water bottle requires three times the amount of water that is needed to fill it.

About 40 percent of bottled water originated as tap water.

It could take over one thousand years for a plastic bottle to biodegrade (naturally decompose).

Plastic bottles contains chemicals called plasticizers, or *phthalates* (pronounced THAL-ates). These seep into the water over time, posing health risks such as hormone disruption and cancer.

In summary, the environmental impacts of plastic-bottled water are impossible to ignore. They include:

- huge oil resources are used to create the bottles

- water resources are depleted in local communities where water is harvested

- health risks are associated with water that isn't as strictly regulated as tap water

- toxic chemicals such as phthalates seep into the water from the plastic

- a large volume of waste is generated and usually not recycled

How Can the Plastic Water Bottle Problem Be Solved?

1. "What if I just reuse one plastic bottle for a while before buying a new one?"
   Not so fast. Reusing plastic bottles often means that more and more phthalates are released into the liquid inside. As previously noted, phthalates have been shown to cause cancer and disrupt bodily hormones. In addition, plastic bottles can harbor harmful bacterial growth inside any cracks or crevices that may form over time.

Remember that sodas, sports drinks, and juices are also bottled "water." Instead of using a disposable plastic bottle, invest in a reusable stainless steel one. If you do buy a plastic bottle, always recycle it, or use it as a water-saving device in your toilet (see page 26).

2. "What about buying in bulk—two liters at a time instead of twelve ounces?"
   This can help reduce the waste, although it doesn't eliminate the oil and water depletion issues or the health concerns.

3. "Let's recycle all the bottles!"
   Again, this is necessary to help reduce waste, but it still won't address other concerns. Also, recycling water bottles requires a lot of energy resources and—you guessed it—water.

4. "Let's make the water bottle companies adhere to stricter water quality standards."
   This could help decrease the health risks from the water, but not from the phthalates in the plastic bottle. Also, it could lead to higher production costs, which could make the bottles of water even more expensive.

5. "How about just . . . not buying so much bottled water?"
   At the core of the water bottle issue is a simple case of supply and demand. If consumers (like you and me) cut back on the purchasing of plastic water bottles—instead drinking water from nonplastic containers—what might happen to the supply? It will sit in warehouses, unsold, which means companies will likely stop manufacturing so many bottles.

So, what *are* people in the real world—teens in particular—doing about this issue?

TEENS IN ACTION

Chagrin Falls, Ohio, United States
Go Green—Drink Tap

In Chagrin Falls, Ohio, the youth board of Community Partnerships for Youth created an awareness campaign about the destructive nature of disposable water bottles culminating in a Go Green Water Tasting. Stationed in a shopping center, the kids invited passersby to taste two water samples, choose the one they liked best, and then guess which sample was bottled water and which came from the tap. The tasters overall preferred tap water and guessed incorrectly that it was bottled water. Students gave out *Go Green—Drink Tap* T-shirts, bumper stickers, and reusable water bottles. Sharing facts in the community and in school raised awareness that not only is tap water better for the environment, it may also taste better than bottled water.

Okanogan, Washington, United States
GEAR UP for Recycling

What do you do if your school sells drinks in plastic bottles but doesn't offer a way to recycle the empties? You GEAR UP for recycling. The GEAR UP program was planned, budgeted, implemented, and presented by sophomores at Okanogan High School in Washington. They set out to educate students, parents, and community members on the importance of recycling plastic bottles and the harmful effects on the environment when recycling does not take place. By educating the community and city council, they spearheaded a plastic bottle recycling program in their school and community.

YOUR TURN

Set Up a Hydration Station

Stainless steel, aluminum, canvas, or glass reusable water bottles are a wonderful and environmentally friendly alternative to single-use plastic water bottles, but they don't do any good unless there's somewhere people can fill them up. You can research, fundraise for, and install a hydration station at your school or in your community. Visit climategen.org and search "Hydration Station" to find an action plan and a list of possible grants you could apply for to fund your project from students at Central High School in St. Paul, Minnesota.

Want to learn more about the problem with single-use water bottles and real solutions? Watch the video "The Story of Bottled Water" at storyofstuff.org.

Where's the Water in Your Backyard?

Think of your own backyard—your community. Can you see the water flowing or rippling in a river, a creek, a pond, a lake, or an ocean? Or is it invisible, churning underground, resting in a marsh, or swirling in a hidden reservoir? Water is continually on the move, all around you. What's the connection between all the different ways that water travels? **Watersheds.** The entire planet is a watershed in which all the water eventually ends up in the ocean. But within this giant watershed are thousands of smaller ones, all working together.

> A **watershed** is an area of land where all the water that is under it or drains off of it flows into the same place.

Watersheds are everywhere and come in many sizes and shapes. They flow between city, state, and national boundaries. In the United States and Puerto Rico, there are 2,267 watersheds.

Knowing about your watershed matters. It helps you take care of your corner of the ecosystem.

Watersheds are very busy places. They create diverse habitats for all kinds of animals—both large and microscopic. They react to various weather conditions, cope with soil erosion, and deal with the impacts of choices made by humans every day. Any new construction project changes a watershed and may disrupt a family of beavers or prevent tadpoles from becoming frogs. Paving over a pond with cement for a parking lot can cause confusion for migrating animals. How we develop and live in our communities can create a big disturbance.

In addition to these more localized watersheds, 114 major land watersheds of the world cover multiple countries and parts of entire continents.

And to make matters even more interesting, our planet can be divided according to *ocean* watersheds.

But however you look at it, the most important fact is this: the watersheds that you depend on for all your daily water needs also depend on *you*—to preserve the habitats, to keep the areas clean and free of pollution, to allow animals to thrive, and to enjoy the beauty of our natural world.

YOUR TURN

Know Your Watershed

Do some action research. What does your local watershed look like? What waterways are closest to you? Find out—and add more to the list!

- Creek
- Lake
- Pond
- Ocean
- Sea
- River
- Canal

- Aquifer (groundwater well or spring)
- Estuary (bay, lagoon, or river mouth)
- Salt marsh (seawater swamp)
- Stream
- Wetland (freshwater swamp)
- Other?

Begin to look for clues about how your waters are interconnected. How? Get out there and explore. Find the waterway closest to your home, school, or community center, and follow along its perimeter to examine how it connects to other water sources. You might be surprised about what you find. Then, create a diagram that shows this interconnectivity—be inventive! Mix photos and illustrations. Insert a picture of what you found along the water's edge. Use this to inform others and inspire them to learn more.

Your Piece of the Watershed

Let's examine watersheds more closely by looking at different parts of this ecological puzzle. Along the way, be thinking of ways you can investigate a community need and take action.

Rivers and Creeks

Rivers and creeks are made of freshwater, usually beginning on a hill or mountain. The headwater, or river source at its highest elevation, might be a single small stream. However, as the river flows downstream, more water gathers from springs, rain, runoff, other rivers and streams, and basically any water that happens to come along for the ride. Can you imagine all the uses rivers serve? From crop irrigation to transportation, recreation, food, and energy, rivers keep industry going, crops growing, and people moving.

In North America, the largest watershed is the Mississippi River basin. Every continent has rivers except for one. Can you guess which one? (See answer at the bottom of this page.)

The World's Most Endangered Rivers

Endangered rivers are not always the most polluted; they may also be rivers that developers and industries are in the process of making important decisions about. The term "endangered" means that if the wrong decisions are made, these rivers may be damaged and made unfit for wildlife to live in them, for animals and humans to drink, or for crop irrigation. Some decisions may even change the way the whole watershed operates or lead to the elimination of the river altogether. As shown in the following charts, these decisions typically involve water removal, dams, overdevelopment, pollution, industry, or climate change.

Remember, water equals *life*. These rivers are at risk, which means the people around them are at risk of losing their livelihoods as well as their daily water supply. Animal life is at risk too. In the past few decades alone, over 20 percent of the planet's 10,000 freshwater fish species have become extinct or endangered.

Answer: Antarctica.

The Top 10 Endangered Rivers in the United States

River	Location	Primary Threat
Colorado River	Arizona, California, Colorado, Nevada, New Mexico, Utah, Wyoming	Climate change, outdated management
Snake River	Washington, Oregon, Idaho	Too many dams
Mobile River	Alabama	Coal ash pollution
Maine's Atlantic Salmon Rivers (Kennebec River, Penobscot River, and Union River)	Maine	Too many dams
Coosa River	Alabama, Georgia	Pollution from poultry farms, habitat loss
Mississippi River	Minnesota, Wisconsin, Iowa, Illinois, Missouri, Kentucky, Tennessee, Arkansas, Mississippi, Louisiana	Pollution, habitat loss
Lower Kern River	California	Excessive water withdrawals
San Pedro River	Arizona	Excessive groundwater pumping, poorly planned development
Los Angeles River	California	Poor management, climate change, pollution
Tar Creek	Oklahoma	Pollution from mining

The Top 10 Endangered Rivers in the World

River	Location	Primary Threat
Salween	Southeast Asia	Too many dams
Danube	Europe	Poor navigation infrastructure
La Plata	South America	Too many dams and poor navigation infrastructure
Rio Grande—Rio Bravo	Southern United States and Mexico	Water over-extraction
Ganges	South and Central Asia	Water over-extraction
Indus	South and Central Asia	Climate change
Nile—Lake Victoria	Africa	Climate change
Murray—Darling	Australia	Invasive species
Mekong	Southeast Asia	Overfishing
Yangtze	China	Pollution

Estuaries

An estuary is a semi-enclosed coastal body of water connected to the open sea that includes a mix of freshwater and seawater. Common estuaries include bays, harbors, inlets, lagoons, river mouths, and wetlands. Throughout history, we have depended on estuaries for trade, food, and shelter from the unpredictable open ocean water. Two major US estuaries, the Chesapeake Bay and San Francisco Bay, are home to large economically and militarily important harbors where many ships pass each year.

Mr. Trash Wheel

Jones Falls is the largest tributary flowing into Baltimore's Inner Harbor, on the Patapsco River. It is also the main source of harbor pollution. John Kellet, the former director of Baltimore's maritime museum, wanted to stop all this trash from making its way into the harbor and eventually downriver to the Chesapeake Bay and Atlantic Ocean. To do this, he designed a machine to intercept trash at the mouth of Jones Falls. John's invention, Mr. Trash Wheel, was installed in 2014. It is powered by an old-fashioned water wheel and designed to look like a mollusk. Two booms guide trash toward the mouth, where it is carried up a ramp on a conveyor belt and deposited in a dumpster. When the dumpster is full, it is transported to an incineration facility and burned to make electricity. Eventually, the city hopes to sort and recycle the trash.

Mr. Trash Wheel was so effective that the city installed three more trash wheels to keep the inner harbor clean: Professor Trash Wheel on Harris Creek in 2016, Captain Trash Wheel in Masonville Cove in 2018, and Gwynnda the Good Wheel of the West at Gwynns Falls in 2021.

Since Mr. Trash Wheel was installed, the trash wheels have collected over two thousand tons of trash and debris that otherwise would have flowed into the Chesapeake Bay, including more than 830,000 plastic bags, over 12.5 million cigarette butts, over 1 million foam containers, 1.5 million plastic bottles, nearly 6,000 sports balls, one keg, a guitar, and a living ball python. You can follow Mr. Trash Wheel and the rest of the Trash Wheel family on Instagram @ mrtrashwheel.

Estuaries are home to a large variety of plants and animals that we depend on for food. Huge numbers of commercially valuable fish from the ocean seek out estuaries to spawn in the protected waters. Oysters, clams, and other shellfish thrive in bays and inlets, as do many species of crabs.

Any trash or sediment in a river naturally ends up in an estuary, since the current of the river slows there due to widening or merging with the ocean's tide. This pollution can have long-term impacts on the health of an estuary. Chemical contaminants can linger in bottom sediments for years, which has caused many areas to be closed for fishing until the chemical has broken down. Excessive loads of silt and other sediments caused by erosion can suffocate bottom-dwelling plants and animals. In addition, disruption of the flow of a river due to damming and irrigation can cause salty water to progress upstream and threaten freshwater species.

Development is another danger estuaries face. Rising human populations are looking for places to expand, and what was once considered marginal land is sometimes now economically valuable. Wetlands are being filled in and mangrove swamps destroyed for housing and industrial purposes—an estimated 215 million acres of the world's estuaries have been lost this way. Not only do we lose a primary habitat for many animals and plants, but we also lose an important buffer zone. Wetlands are remarkably good at using plants and microbes to break down chemical compounds and metals from runoff pollution. They also help trap carbon and are important in the fight against climate change. Finally, estuaries often act as crucial storm barriers in places such as the Louisiana bayou.

Shelter from the Storm

For years prior to Hurricane Katrina in 2005, oil and gas companies and private developers had been tunneling through and paving over the wetlands that separated New Orleans and surrounding communities from the Gulf of Mexico. Without this natural shelter zone fully intact, the devastation caused by Katrina was far worse in these cities than it might otherwise have been.

Visit epa.gov/wetlands for more information about how you can get involved in restoring crucial wetlands.

TEENS IN ACTION

Luanda, Angola
The Mangrove Project

Mangroves are a vital part of the ecosystem inside the Peninsula de Mussulo on the coast of Belas, Angola. These trees provide protection for the shoreline, as well as a source of income and building materials for locals. Mangrove swamps are also home to countless plants, animals, sea life, and microorganisms, but they are being destroyed to make room for urban development.

students transplanting mangrove propagules

photo credit: EarthEcho International

Students at Luanda International School saw the deforestation of mangrove swamps in their local community, and they wanted to do something about it. They partnered with environmental group OTCHIVA to help plant new trees and restore this important ecosystem. The students performed in-depth research on water salinity and the zonation of mangroves to gain a better understanding of these trees' optimal growing conditions. Their research informed their efforts and helped them successfully reforest large areas and restore native plants and flowers.

Lakes

Oh, go jump in the lake! But wait . . . is the lake clean? Have pollutants been building over time from boating or shipping traffic or industrial waste? Does the lake even have water in it? By definition, a lake is a body of (usually) freshwater surrounded by land. It is larger than a pond, has a river that feeds it, and is not directly a part of the ocean. However, a lake can also be a dry basin waiting for water to fill it in seasonally.

What creates a lake? Landslides, glaciers, sinkholes, a slow-moving river bend, or a volcanic crater that fills with precipitation—these are just a few origins of lakes. We humans have made our share of lakes by building dams or diverting water sources for irrigation or drinking water reservoirs. Once in existence, lakes continually change through erosion, climate changes, and human use.

Lake Superior Beaches Closed Due to Contamination

In recent years, Lake Superior beaches in Duluth, Minnesota, frequently have been closed in summer due to high amounts of bacteria, including E. coli, in the water. The primary sources of the bacteria appear to be nearby wastewater treatment plants and feces contamination of migrating water birds such as terns, geese, and gulls. This is just one example of a growing trend of US beach closings—in both lakes and coastal areas—due to pollution. In the 2018 swimming season, the Environmental Protection Agency reported that 38 percent of the beaches they were monitoring had one or more advisories or closures.

Before visiting a beach near you, investigate its water quality by visiting epa.gov and searching "Beaches."

a beach closed due to chemical pollution of the water

Think of a lake you live by or care about. This lake, like all lakes, needs to be clean and safe for the animals and plants that inhabit its water and the surrounding area. Sadly this is not always the case. Recreation, agriculture, mining, and other activities can disrupt the health of these crucial water systems.

Do You Know Your Lake Facts?
(See answers at the bottom of this page.)

1. Which country has more than 60 percent of the world's lakes?

2. Which country is known as "The Land of the Thousand Lakes"?

3. Which of the fifty United States is known as "The Land of Ten Thousand Lakes"?

4. Which Canadian province boasts 100,000 lakes?

TEENS IN ACTION

Chicago, Illinois, United States
Calumet Is My Backyard

The Lake Calumet region of Chicago is situated in the Lake Michigan watershed. During the early twentieth century, Lake Calumet was home to major industrial development. Since that time, most of the steel mills have closed, leaving degraded natural areas behind especially susceptible to invasive species (often called "weeds") like dogwood, buckthorn, and garlic mustard. That's where CIMBY comes in, which stands for Calumet Is My Backyard, a partnership between schools and local organizations. CIMBY connects high school environmental science students with opportunities to be stewards in the Lake Calumet area of Chicago's southeast side. Throughout the year students adopt one of Calumet's natural sites—wetlands, prairies, forest preserves, savannah woodlands, marshes—and put their

Canada, Finland, Minnesota, Manitoba

learning to use. Over the years, students have built trails, solved erosion problems, gathered seeds for planting, tested and monitored water quality, examined biodiversity factors, and provided general stewardship to support their adopted site. As for the invasive species, students work together to remove these plants and reintroduce native species to the area. They are saving their neighborhood's entire ecosystem!

Kenya
Bring Back Lake Victoria

Lake Victoria is the second-largest freshwater lake in the world, but plastic pollution is harming its waters and the plants, animals, and people who depend on them. Siblings Michelle and Jeremy Muchilwa launched their organization Bring Back Lake Victoria to address this pollution. After spending months doing research and talking with

Lake Victoria, Kenya

various government institutions, they discovered a big problem: there was a lack of data about how much plastic was polluting the lake and where it was coming from, which made it hard to find solutions. They decided to find the data themselves using citizen science! The created an app called Ziwa Safi where users provide information about where, what kind, and how much plastic they found, and then the app offers information about nearby recycling centers where people can dispose of the plastic gathered in their cleanup.

Turning Back Time
In your region, what event in history left a problem to be solved? Research an industry that may have had a local impact and what was done to remedy the situation. How has your community responded to ecological problems in the past? And, most importantly, what can you do now? Local libraries, historical societies, and environmental groups can provide information and guidance and may already have action plans in place that you can join.

Coastal Areas

What do you like to do at the ocean shore? Surf, sunbathe, build giant sandcastles, picnic, swim, fish, sail, kayak, hike, camp? Beaches offer us adventure, play, and relaxation. While you may be out bodysurfing, others are working to make this possible. In fact, entire cities, regions, and countries depend on the money tourists spend while visiting their ocean shores.

Erosion, the wearing away of rock and soil, is a major creative force of many beaches. Erosion provides sand for new beaches and the maintenance of old ones. Erosion forms the stacks and arches found along rocky coastlines, and it provides the materials that form deltas and barrier islands. A certain amount of erosion is natural and necessary. But what happens when people try to control these shifting sands and build permanent structures, such as houses, restaurants, shops, and hotels, close to the shore? Then, erosion becomes a problem. Beaches can disappear over time, or even overnight during severe storms.

Of all the types of pollution that beaches endure, oil spills are perhaps the most deadly. A layer of thick oil quickly smothers most small animals, and larger animals that get away are poisoned soon after. Beaches do recover over time, but decades may pass before new communities of plants and animals migrate back to an affected area.

a dead oiled guillemot found during the Erika oil spill in France, 1999

photo credit: Sascha Regmann/Project Blue Sea/Marine Photobank

Oil + Water = A Poisonous Mess

On April 20, 2010, the *Deepwater Horizon* oil rig exploded in the Gulf of Mexico. Eleven people died, and millions of barrels of oil spilled into the Gulf. The oil reached the shores of Texas, Louisiana, Mississippi, Alabama, and Florida. The United States government, environmental groups, businesses, and concerned people have all taken action to help clean up this oily mess.

More than a decade has passed since the *Deepwater Horizon* disaster, but scientists, volunteers, and teens are still working to restore important coastal habitats that were affected. In the process of restoring the coast, scientists discovered another oil spill from a destroyed oil platform that had been leaking since 2004! It had gone undetected for six years until monitoring for contamination from *Deepwater Horizon* revealed abandoned leaking oil wells buried on the seafloor. Thanks to the Gulf cleanup efforts, that spill has also been contained.

Ongoing projects to restore and protect the Gulf include building and restoring barrier islands, designating some marine and coastal areas as legally protected, replenishing marshes and swamps, restoring oyster reefs, and building living shorelines to protect coastlines from rising sea levels.

❝ The oil that gets dispersed into the water will have consequences and impacts on this area for decades to come. Anyone who thinks otherwise is just not paying attention. There's still oil from the Exxon Valdez oil spill twenty years ago in Prince William Sound. These things don't go away. ❞

—Philippe Cousteau, speaking about the BP oil spill in the Gulf of Mexico in April 2010

Other kinds of pollution take their toll on beaches as well. Garbage that washes up on shore can strangle, entrap, or poison wildlife. Sea turtles, for example, often mistake plastic bags for jellyfish, and many have died as a result of eating the bags. Industrial waste is often fatal to many kinds of sea life as well. Sunscreens, perfumes, and body lotions wash off people's skin as they play and swim, and chemicals from medicines, plastics, batteries, and other products can enter our waters when people don't dispose of these items properly. Raw sewage has caused dangerous algal blooms (toxic algae colonies), and, along with excessive fertilizer runoff, contributes to the formation of deadly "red tides," where the water is colored red by huge numbers of poisonous algal blooms. These algal blooms have been partly responsible for an increase in "dead zones," or coastal areas that once supported abundant marine life but have become so oxygen-depleted they are now lifeless. Scientists have identified 415 dead zones worldwide, the largest nearly covering the 63,700-square-mile Gulf of Oman in the Arabian Sea.

TEENS IN ACTION

Honolulu, Hawai'i, United States
Preserving Ka'ena Point

Jutting out from the westernmost tip of O'ahu, Ka'ena Point is a sacred site. Early Hawai'ians revered the rugged and remote area as a place where departing spirits leapt into the ancestral realm. Today, Ka'ena Point is a fifty-nine-acre state-owned nature reserve, and it remains one of Hawai'i's last coastal ecosystems, harboring nesting seabirds, monk seals, and native plants. However, after decades of overuse by visitors and rutting by four-wheel-drive vehicles, the sand dunes of Ka'ena Point are rapidly eroding into the sea.

"We felt if we could plant seeds, both literally and metaphorically, the kids could go back year after year and see the fruit of their labor."
—Dave Blanchette, Punahou School teacher

"It feels good to give back to the environment. When people come back in later years, they will see a better place and it's good to know that we helped make it better."—Chasen, age 14

Eighth graders at Punahou School in Honolulu became part of a community effort to preserve and restore this endangered coastline. Teams started off by planting seedlings of native plants along a scarred section of the dunes. They hoped the plants would halt the erosion and restore the pristine natural habitat.

For many students, this was their first visit to Ka'ena Point. "It was such a remote place; everything looked perfect, and it was just us and a couple of people fishing," marveled Chasen, age fourteen. "We had to be peaceful and mindful of this place." After offering a traditional Hawai'ian chant, the students went to work constructing a protective sand barrier, planting the seeds along eroded gullies, and posting signs to prohibit vehicles. The students collectively planted two hundred seedlings. "We had a lot of teamwork," said Jackie, age fourteen, describing the coordinated effort to lug gallons of water, mulch, and plants across the dry landscape. Chasen agreed that the physical challenge of the half-day hike brought the students closer together.

photo credit: Dario Salgado

Ka'ena Point, Hawai'i

SUMMARY

Investigation. By investigating, you've learned the facts, read the stories, and heard the results. Investigation helps clarify what is going on around you—especially the underlying issues, the history, and the causes. At the same time, doing investigation introduces you to possible service partners, raises your own awareness, and shows where action is needed. Perhaps most of all, it helps you discover your own unique skills and talents that you will bring into the world of doing service.

photo credit: David Makepeace

STAGE 2

DIVE IN→PREPARE

You have investigated and chosen the community water need you want to address. Now it's time to move on to the second stage of your "Going Blue" journey: preparing yourself for action by gaining an in-depth understanding of the larger water system you aim to help.

The Story of Tar Creek: Part 2

Miami, Oklahoma, United States

How Did They Prepare?

Through regular classes like science and English and extracurricular work, students conducted extensive research on a range of topics including water contamination and the results of human exposure to toxic heavy metals, namely lead. They learned about the causes and effects of **lead poisoning** in humans and animals. They tested Tar Creek waters. They asked experts at major universities and in government and tribal councils for more information about repairing the land and protecting the community. They wanted to find out if fish would ever swim in Tar Creek again.

Lead Poisoning

- Human exposure to high levels of lead is extremely toxic and can be fatal.

- People can get lead in their bodies by breathing or swallowing lead dust.

- Lead exposure can harm young children and babies even before they are born.

- Even children who seem healthy can have high levels of lead in their bodies.

The Story of Tar Creek continues on page 108.

Tar Creek sampling photo credit: University of Oklahoma School of Civil Engineering and Environmental Science

The Amazing Ocean

To fully understand the issues faced in the planet's waterways—from Miami, Oklahoma, to Cairo, Egypt, to Sydney, Australia—you first need to understand what's happening at the hub of all these waterways: the ocean.

If you think of the planet's streams, creeks, lakes, and rivers as the veins in our bodies, the ocean is our heart where all the waters meet. With the following facts, stories, and words of wisdom from people who care deeply about this watery heart, you will be poised to dive in. Are you ready? Take a deep breath . . .

The ocean supplies over half of Earth's oxygen.

Earth has one big, connected ocean with many ocean basins, such as the Atlantic, Pacific, Indian, Arctic, and Southern.

Ninety-seven percent of Earth's water is in the ocean.

Ocean life ranges in size from the smallest living organism, a virus, to the largest animal that has ever lived on Earth, the blue whale.

The ocean provides food, medicines, minerals, energy resources, jobs, and transportation of goods and people, and plays a role in many countries' national security. It also plays a role in many cultural and religious practices and ceremonies, and has influenced literature, visual arts, poetry, film, theater, and music.

Nearly half of the world's population lives in coastal areas.

The ocean covers about 70 percent of the planet's surface.

"Every time you step off the land into the liquid—into the ocean—you're traveling somewhere very few people venture. You've immediately embarked on a great adventure."—*Tierney Thys, marine biologist*

The Carbon Conundrum:
Part #1—Ocean Acidification

The three main threats to the health of our oceans today are ocean acidification, climate change, and pollution. Of these three, two are caused by a common enemy: carbon, which exists in water and air primarily as the gas carbon dioxide, or CO_2.

You've likely heard a lot about climate change in the news and you know by now how burning fossil fuels threatens our environment by trapping heat in the atmosphere, creating greenhouse gases. One of these gases is CO_2, created mainly by burning coal and oil to power factories, cars, and farms. But what you might not know is that CO_2 can also damage our oceans by causing ocean acidification. Increasing CO_2 levels in our environment changes the ocean's chemistry. As the ocean is forced to absorb increasing amounts of carbon, the ocean's **pH level** decreases and the water becomes more and more acidic.

The ocean has absorbed about a third of the carbon that we've spewed into the atmosphere since the Industrial Revolution began over two hundred years ago. For a while many people thought this was a good thing—better in the oceans than in the air, right? *Wrong.* Scientists later realized that when the ocean becomes acidic, calcium extraction from the water becomes difficult for sea creatures that depend on this calcium to build their shells, like coral, crabs, oysters, and lobsters. What happens if they are left without the defenses of their shells? They die, and the ocean food web is severely disrupted. That's bad news for all of us.

> **pH Level**
>
> Water everywhere carries nutrients, oxygen, and biochemicals from place to place. The amount of acid in water can be measured by a scale called pH, which stands for "potential hydrogen." A low pH number indicates high acidity, while a high pH number means low acidity. The pH scale runs from 0 to 14, with 7 being neutral. Ocean water typically has a pH level of around 8, which means it's a base, not an acid, although it is growing more acidic.

Food Web, Interrupted

Increased carbon pollution causes a rise in our ocean's acid levels, which affects the overall health of the ocean ... and may disrupt the entire planet's dinner, a.k.a. the food web. Earth's food web is made up of all its living organisms—from bacteria to plants to fish to pigs to humans—that depend on each other as food sources to survive.

Here is a brief summary of how carbon pollution affects the food web:

- Ocean water absorbs the CO_2 released into the air when we burn fossil fuels.

- This causes the pH in the water to decrease, making the water more acidic.

- The acidic water affects small sea creatures by weakening their protective shells, which leads to their deaths.

- When the smaller creatures die, less food is available for the larger fish to eat, so they die too.

- All of this equals less fish for bears, humans, and other mammals to eat.

Here are some specific examples:

The tiny mollusk *Limacina helicina* (called a "sea butterfly") found in Arctic waters is especially vulnerable to the acidification process. Whales, salmon, herring, and various seabirds dine on this little shellfish. Its disappearance would therefore have a major impact on the entire ocean food web.

The cold-water coral species *Lophelia pertusa* is also extremely vulnerable to rising acidity. Reefs in the northern oceans are made up of only one or two kinds of coral, unlike tropical reefs, which are made up of many different kinds. The loss of Lophelia pertusa would therefore devastate coral reefs off the coasts of Norway and Scotland, damaging the habitats of dozens of fish species and other sea creatures.

sea butterfly
photo credit: NOAA

The Carbon Conundrum:
Part #2—Climate Change

Like acidification, climate change is caused, in part, by humans pumping tons of carbon gas into the atmosphere. When CO_2 and other greenhouse gases—nitrous oxide, methane, and ozone—are released into the air in large quantities, they create a barrier (like a blanket) around our planet that traps solar radiation and shoots it back to the earth. This causes the earth to slowly heat up, which messes with all kinds of things . . . including the ocean.

The Krill-Carbon Cycle

A lot of people believe that humanity's large-scale disruption of the carbon cycle started with our use of coal, oil, and gas as drivers of economic growth. This is not true. Our disruption of the global carbon cycle actually began hundreds of years earlier, during the seventeenth century, when whaling became a major industry in North America. The primary use of whales was for whale oil to power lights, though their baleen were also prized for making corsets and hoop skirts.

For hundreds of years, North American—and to a lesser extent European and Scandinavian—whalers crisscrossed the ocean, killing millions of whales. You might be wondering what this has to do with the carbon cycle. Well, whales are an enormous carbon sink. In other words, they absorb and store carbon in their bodies. It is estimated that one whale can remove carbon from the environment equivalent to the amount removed by 1,500 trees. Whales then store that carbon in their bodies, and when they die, they sink and bring it with them to the ocean floor.

But whales have an even more important role in helping sequester billions of tons of carbon in the deep ocean each year, with the help of two little creatures: krill and phytoplankton. Krill are tiny crustaceans that live throughout the ocean but are most abundant in the southern ocean around Antarctica. Krill are the central character in the world's largest carbon cycle, and it all comes down to poop. You see, krill eat phytoplankton—tiny, plant-like creatures that live at the surface of the open ocean. Phytoplankton create energy through photosynthesis, and that process includes absorbing carbon out of the atmosphere and emitting oxygen back into the atmosphere.

Phytoplankton are responsible for generating 50 percent of the oxygen on Earth. But they also hold the carbon they sequester in their tissue. After krill eat phytoplankton, their poop carries that carbon with it as it sinks to the bottom of the ocean. In this way, krill inadvertently sequester billions of tons of carbon a year in the deep ocean by doing something as simple and fundamental as pooping. But it doesn't stop there! Krill are, in turn, a key food source for whales, which can hold the carbon from the krill in their bodies for up to 100 years until they die. And it keeps going! Whale poop (Who would have thought it all comes down to poop?) is rich in iron. That iron is a critical compound needed by phytoplankton to grow.

All this means that when whalers killed millions of whales, they caused populations of phytoplankton to crash, along with these creatures' critical carbon-sequestering functions (remember, BILLIONS of tons a year). Without enough phytoplankton, krill populations crashed, which in turn hurt not just the remaining whale populations, but also all the other creatures that eat krill, like penguins, seals, and fish. So, in addition to disrupting the global carbon cycle centuries before people thought, humanity started destroying the ocean food web at a large scale a lot sooner too.

The Global Conveyor Belt

When the ocean heats up during global warming, this affects how its currents flow. Currents operate according to a process called *thermohaline circulation*—or what is commonly known as the "global conveyor belt."

Here is what the ocean's conveyor belt looks like:

Thermohaline circulation is the rising and sinking of ocean water driven by contrasts in water density, which is due in turn to differences in temperature and salinity.

On the relatively warm surface of the ocean, wind moves the currents along. But currents flow at all depths of the ocean. The force that drives the current in deeper, colder water is water density, and the density is controlled by the water's temperature (thermo) and saltiness, or salinity (haline). Combine them and you have thermohaline circulation.

Here is how the ocean's conveyor belt operates:

1. Water freezes in the Polar Regions—forming sea ice.

2. This ice forms using freshwater, leaving the salt behind and making the surrounding ocean water saltier.

3. The density, or weight, of the water gets heavier because of the salt, and the water starts to sink.

4. The warmer water on the ocean's surface replaces the sinking water, and soon this water gets cold and salty, and it too begins to sink.

5. This is the start of the deep-ocean currents driving the conveyor belt.

The global thermohaline circulation moves all over the ocean, from Antarctica to the equator to Africa, South America, North America, the Indian Ocean, and the Pacific Ocean. It acts as a giant heating and air-conditioning system, providing warmth and cooling for our planet. For example, the sinking cold, salty, dense water in the North Atlantic Ocean helps draw warm surface waters northward. Heat from the ocean rises into the atmosphere above the North Atlantic Ocean, and winds carry the heat east, making Europe warmer. In addition to our weather, this process also impacts our food sources. Cool, nutrient-rich waters support the growth of algae and seaweed, which is a key ingredient in the food web we depend upon.

time for
REFLECTION

What have you already learned about oceans that you did not know before? What do you most want to remember? Who do you want to talk with about what you're learning? Share the news—be a voice for change!

"I'm Melting!"

As you've likely heard, global warming is also causing Earth's glaciers to melt faster than predicted. In fact, by some estimates, Glacier National Park in Montana could be without glaciers by the year 2030, and the entire Arctic Ocean may have ice-free periods as early as 2035. What will all this melting ice do to our rivers and lakes, oceans and shores? To our plants and animals? To our climate? To us?

an iceberg visible above and below the water's surface

Our Polar Regions are particularly susceptible to global warming. Arctic temperatures have been rising twice as fast as elsewhere in the world. On the Antarctic Peninsula, temperatures have increased five times faster. These regions are particularly sensitive to warming, in part, because of two persistent cycles:

Cycle #1: Ice and snow reflect the majority of the solar energy reaching the earth's surface, while ice-free surfaces absorb this energy. Snow and ice cover therefore have a cooling effect on the earth, but as they melt, more solar energy is absorbed, raising temperatures and melting even *more* ice.

Cycle #2: As ice melts in these regions, the permafrost (permanently frozen ground) thaws. Permafrost contains carbon that has been trapped in the soil since the last ice age, over a million years ago. As the permafrost melts, large quantities of carbon are released in the form of methane, a powerful greenhouse gas that increases global warming.

All this melting ice releases freshwater into the salty oceans, which can disrupt the thermohaline circulation—the global conveyor belt. Salty ocean water at high latitudes is becoming fresher as polar ice melts, and this lighter fresh water is not sinking and circulating through the deep ocean as it should. Given the current rate of change, scientists estimate that the global ocean conveyor belt may slow or stop altogether within the next few decades. This would have serious implications for countries in the northern hemisphere, as the warm surface waters in the Atlantic cease to be moved northward, and could eventually send Western Europe and North America into a deep freeze.

The Power of Water

Pour water into your hands and it seems oh-so-gentle. Dive into a pool—how refreshing! Stand in the way of a typhoon, however, and you will experience the real power of water. How does ocean warming lead to these types of dangerous weather conditions? An increase in ocean temperatures, as we've seen, can disrupt the global thermohaline circulation, which in turn can affect the oceans' tides and storm systems. As humans continue down this destructive path, hurricanes, typhoons, and other tropical storms will continue to increase in number, frequency, and intensity.

time for REFLECTION

What natural disasters have been in the news lately? How might they confirm that our climate conditions are changing? Take the information from these pages and relate it to what's happening today in the world around you. Stay connected!

Climate Refugees

Populations migrate for various reasons: to find new jobs, to be closer to family, to escape war, and to pursue an education, among many others. But did you ever think people would move because of climate change? A new term is being used for this phenomenon: **climate refugees**. These are people forced to leave their homes due to the impact of global warming. Already about one-fifth of the 12,000 residents of Tuvalu, a tiny island nation in the South Pacific, have migrated, primarily to New Zealand, because of rising seas, more frequent dangerous storms, and the destruction of coral reefs that are the backbone of the islands. Other regions are being studied by scientists concerned with vulnerable populations, such as the deltas of Vietnam, the coast of Bangladesh, and the Sahel in Africa; these areas are faced with flooding, rising sea levels, or water shortages. The international think tank the Institute for Economics and Peace predicts that by 2050, the number of climate refugees worldwide could surge to over one billion.

"It is interesting how often the impact of climate change is illustrated by talking about the problems the polar bears will face, rather than the much greater number of poor people who will die unless significant investments are made to help them."

—Bill Gates, founder of Microsoft, philanthropist

Learn About a Threatened Area

Select a place in the world at risk of losing its very existence, like Tuvalu. Or choose a place that might succumb to drought, such as the African Sahel, or be destroyed by flooding, like the deltas in Vietnam. Learn all you can about the issue. Make a commitment to follow this area's progress over time. Discover different viewpoints and courses of action proposed by governments, local and outside communities, and area businesses. See how the media covers the story. Become an expert, and then share your knowledge with others.

Plastics, Pollution & Trash

Okay, so carbon pollution = ocean acidification + global warming = a huge problem. But carbon is certainly not the only thing we're dumping into our environment. A full 80 percent of pollution in the marine environment comes from land-based sources, such as chemical fertilizers, waste products, and litter.

Remember that granola bar wrapper you accidentally dropped on the ground over lunch? It might arrive at the beach before you do. Litter can travel to the ocean from many miles inland, blown by the wind or carried along by rivers and streams. We are all responsible for food wrappers, bottles, and bags in our waters. Overflowing sewage systems and storm drains add to the burden by ferrying trash from roads and streets to the sea. Marine debris these days includes mainly synthetic materials, such as plastics, where it once contained mostly organic materials. Items like packing straps, tarps, nets, and containers last for years and often travel thousands of miles on ocean currents.

This sea lion became entangled in a gill net and was cut free. However, the monofilament lines around its head and neck were not removed. As the animal grew, the line cut a deep gash into its skin. Hundreds of thousands of sea lions and other wildlife become entangled in discarded fishing gear each year.

photo credit: Marine Photobank from © 1990 Bob Talbot, LegaSea Project

Bioaccumulation is the gradual buildup of a chemical in a living organism. This happens because 1) the chemical piles up faster than it can be metabolized, or 2) the chemical simply can't be metabolized. If this chemical is toxic to the organism, then the buildup becomes a health concern. Common toxic chemicals come from plastics, pesticides used on farm crops, car emissions, and mercury from coal-burning and other industries.

Trash and plastic swirl through the world's oceans, leaving a trail of destruction. Plastic contains toxic chemicals, and as animals mistake the plastic for food, they are exposed to these toxins, which build up in their systems over time in a process called **bioaccumulation.** Many animals suffocate trying to eat plastic bags or other items. Others starve to death from a lack of nutrition. Even uneaten trash, like nets and plastic soda can rings, ensnares and kills thousands of creatures. Curious seals poke their noses into plastic containers and get stuck, preventing them from eating or breathing. Playful dolphins swirl around discarded fishing rope, becoming entangled. When animals get caught in abandoned fishing nets, lines, and ropes in a phenomenon known as "ghost fishing," they may drown immediately or drag the debris around until they weaken and die. Nets drifting underwater can also snag on corals, sea fans, or sponges, damaging or destroying them.

TEENS IN ACTION

Worldwide
International Coastal Cleanup Day

During the 2020 Ocean Conservancy International Coastal Cleanup, more than 200,000 volunteers worldwide picked up an astounding 5.2 million pounds of trash along an estimated 49,000-plus miles of coastline. Of the items tallied, from light bulbs to fishing line, the top three items recorded were cigarette butts (965,000), beverage bottles (627,000), and food wrappers/containers (574,000). In all, over 8 million items were collected. All these things can be easily contained if people dispose of them carefully. Volunteers also rounded up significant amounts of tiny trash, or items smaller than 2.5 centimeters, including foam pieces (364,000), glass pieces (81,000), and plastic pieces (1.7 million).

The Ocean Conservancy has been collecting data on the International Coastal Cleanup (ICC) for over thirty-five years. Here are some surprising statistics from that time:

- The total weight of trash removed over the past thirty-five years of the ICC is equal to 1,148 blue whales.

- When laid end to end, the straws and stirrers collected would stretch the entire length of the Himalayas (around 1,500 miles).

- Over thirty-five years, volunteers have collected enough plastic grocery bags (over 357 million) to cover 1,196 Olympic-sized swimming pools.

- Since 2017, the top ten most commonly found items have all been plastic (including cigarette butts, which are made of plastic).

- Every year, thousands of marine mammals, sea turtles, seabirds, and fishes are injured or killed because of encounters with common items we carelessly throw away.

Greenville, North Carolina, United States
Team Environmental Droners

Since the COVID-19 pandemic began in 2020, an increase in single-use plastics led to an increase in the amount of trash along the roadways and waterways of Greenville, North Carolina. Two local teens noted that their community is positioned between two major river basins, the Neuse and the Tar Pamlico, thirty miles from the coast. These two rivers flow into critical coastal systems that are vital to fisheries, tourism, and the Atlantic Ocean, and they were carrying all that litter downstream. The teens knew they wanted to do something about this problem as part of EarthEcho's OurEcho Challenge in 2021.

Calling themselves Team Environmental Droners, the teens developed an innovative method of using drones to combat the plastic pollution crisis, global warming, and contamination of local and national waters. Drones were used to spot trash in remote areas and assist in the mobilization of groups to remove the litter. This allowed much better coverage of areas that were collecting trash flowing down rivers and streams. But awareness of the pollution was just the first step. Next, the Environmental Droners integrated even more technology into their clean-up efforts. They developed an innovative trash locating and mapping app called the Litter Locator. The app, developed in partnership with East Carolina University Water Resources Center, allows crowdsourcing of litter cleanups among young people and community members.

COVID-19's Impact on the Ocean

In 2021, the Ocean Conservancy released the first-ever report tracking pollution from personal protective equipment (PPE), such as single-use masks and plastic gloves, and its impact on the ocean. In only six months, coastal cleanup volunteers collected over 100,000 pieces of single-use PPE. On surveys, 94 percent of volunteers reported that they found PPE at a cleanup, and 50 percent reported seeing PPE pollution on a daily basis.

The Great Pacific Garbage Patch

Yuck! The Great Pacific Garbage Patch, Trash Island, Plastic Soup—whatever you call it, there's one heck of a garbage dump floating out in our ocean. Located between Hawai'i and California, it's twice the size of Texas. The mass has been growing since the 1950s, and unless people intervene, this hunk of junk will continue to collect more and more waste—including discarded electronics, children's toys, and most of all, tons of nonbiodegradable plastic.

Of this giant heap, 40 percent is plastic—evidence that humans are doing a lousy job of properly disposing of the 380 million tons of plastic we create every year. We only recycle about 9 percent of that amount. With the garbage patch sprawling in international waters, no country is willing to take responsibility for the massive cleanup necessary. This leaves independent researchers to imagine solutions. One organization, Project Kaisei, suggests harnessing the energy stored in the plastic to create fuel. In the meantime, other researchers are tracking the movement of debris making its way into this trash island.

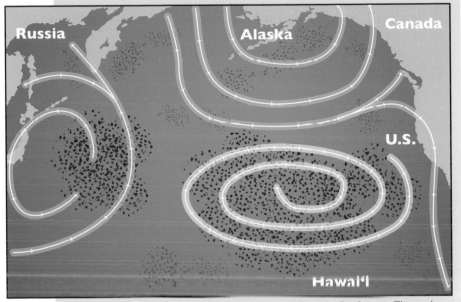

The above map shows how trash enters the ocean along the Pacific coast. The trash swirls in two main vortices: the western Pacific Garbage Patch (on left) and the eastern Pacific Garbage Patch (on right).

Environmental stewards remind consumers that one long-term solution is to change the way our plastics are made. Look for the BPI (Biodegradable Products Institute) logo when deciding what to buy—these products are compostable (able to be composted and broken down into natural elements).

One thing is for certain: if left alone to circulate in our oceans, this garbage will continue to permanently harm the natural environment and contaminate our food supply with the toxins of our own waste.

Whenever possible, avoid buying six-packs of cans and bottles in plastic holders. If you do come across these holders, be sure to cut the plastic rings apart and dispose of them properly, so they don't end up ensnaring an animal by accident.

TEENS IN ACTION

Delft, The Netherlands
The Ocean Cleanup

While scuba diving in Greece, sixteen-year-old Boyan Slat saw more plastic bags than fish. He wondered what could be done about it. This led him to research plastic pollution for a school project, where he learned that no one was making a serious attempt to clean up ocean garbage patches and prevent further pollution at the source. He wondered: *Why was a cleanup so impossible?*

Through research, Boyan learned that using boats and nets to clean up garbage patches would take thousands of years, cost billions of dollars, and be harmful to sea life and the environment. But, he asked, what if humans used the ocean currents to our advantage and let plastic come to us instead of going after it? This idea for a passive concentration system was the result of over a year of experimenting with ideas and performing simple tests. And after graduating high school, Boyan was invited to present his idea at a TEDx conference. His video didn't take off immediately, but eventually it went viral, which gave him the momentum to get his nonprofit organization, The Ocean Cleanup, up and running. The Ocean Cleanup aims to remove 90 percent of floating plastic from the ocean by 2040 and stop plastic pollution at the mouths of rivers before it ever enters the ocean.

In July 2021, The Ocean Cleanup deployed a test of System 002, its first large-scale ocean cleanup system using Boyan's passive concentration idea, in the Great Pacific Garbage Patch. After twelve weeks, the trial run was deemed successful. System 002 will continue to operate in the Great Pacific Garbage Patch while the team at The Ocean Cleanup works to develop a larger system, which eventually will be scaled to a fleet of systems operating together to clean up plastic pollution in the ocean.

Port Macquarie, Australia
Ocean Support

Ever since she was young, Shalise Leesfield and her family have spent nearly all their free time either in or near the ocean. But during these visits, Shalise noticed there were huge clumps of used fishing line and other plastic trash littering the shore. After doing research, Shalise learned that fishing line can be one of the most harmful kinds of trash that makes its way into our waters. Many birds, sea turtles, and other marine animals are injured or killed after becoming tangled in fishing line and its hooks and tackle. So she decided to do something about it.

Shalise learned about a company that sent out free fishing line receptacles. She performed environmental studies of her local beach, where she documented how much fishing line she found. She created a presentation to share her findings with her local council. After seeing Shalise's presentation, the council approved placing two trial bins in the community. The trial was so successful that the council quickly approved the placement of additional bins.

"I believe if you have a passion or you want to pursue something, it really doesn't matter how old you are. Kids should have their voice heard, so make sure you have your voice heard." —Shalise Leesfield

Every week, Shalise empties the bins, but she doesn't just throw all that plastic into a landfill. Instead, Shalise puts the fishing line to a new use. She makes colorful bracelets and sells them to raise money and awareness about the issue of pollution in our waterways.

Shalise also wants to inspire other school-age tweens and teens to do the same, so she created an online school program called Plastic Free Schools where she shares tips, strategies, and audit tools for young people to make change where it is most needed. Most recently, Shalise even worked with Dr. Sylvia Earle to have Fish Rock Cave in Australia declared a Mission Blue Hope Spot—an area deemed critical to the health of the ocean.

West Cork, Ireland
Cleaning Up Microplastics

Did you know that the average human eats about one Lego's worth of plastic each week, and up to forty pounds of plastic in their lifetime? Unlike sea turtles and other animals, humans aren't likely to mistake plastic for food, so how are we eating so much of it? Some of the plastic we ingest is in the form of microplastic particles in drinking water.

As plastic photodegrades, microplastics make their way into drinking water systems. Some of these particles are so tiny that they can't be captured and filtered out with current water treatment methods. One young person, Fionn Ferriera, hopes to change this.

Fionn developed a method for removing microplastics from water using ferrofluid (a magnetic solution) and oil. This microplastic removal method won him the 2019 Google Science Fair when he was eighteen years old. Now in his twenties, Fionn hopes to make microplastic removal a global standard in water treatment.

Does Plastic Biodegrade?

The vast majority of plastic does not biodegrade, or break down into natural elements, like organic materials do. At least not for 1,000 years or more. Rather than biodegrade, plastic **photodegrades**—it breaks into tiny toxic bits. These fragmented particles, called nurdles, cause further problems. They're often ingested by jellyfish and other marine life, who mistake them for food. These creatures are then ingested by other predators, including larger marine animals, birds, animals on land, and humans. In this way, plastic moves through the food web.

An estimated 10 million tons of plastic pollution enter the world's ocean every year. How much trash do you make as one person? Could you make less? Here are some quick ideas to start with:

- Buy products contained in less packaging.
- Buy compostable products whenever possible, and follow your city's recycling guidelines.
- Use a reusable cloth bag when shopping, carry a reusable water bottle to stay hydrated, and skip the straws whenever you can.

 Want to know more about the Great Pacific Garbage Patch and plastic pollution and get involved? Visit these sites:

NOAA's Marine Debris Program: marinedebris.noaa.gov. The Marine Debris Program is part of the National Oceanic and Atmospheric Administration (NOAA), a division of the United States government. The program has funded and helped support over 140 projects working with partners and addressing marine debris across the nation.

Plastic Oceans: plasticoceans.org. Plastic Oceans International is a nonprofit organization whose goal is to end plastic pollution and to foster sustainable communities worldwide. Plastic Oceans aims to inspire and incite action to change consumer behavior, industrial practices, and public policy to create a healthier planet for the future.

"There are no boundaries on the real Planet Earth. No United States, no Soviet Union*, no China, no Taiwan . . . Rivers flow unimpeded across the swaths of continents. The persistent tides—the pulse of the sea—do not discriminate; they push against all the varied shores on Earth."—Jacques Cousteau, explorer

*The Soviet Union ceased to exist in 1991 and the area now includes Russia and several other Eurasian countries.

time for
REFLECTION

Who's in charge here? Since all the world's waterways are inter-connected, can any nation's government look at the Great Pacific Garbage Patch and say, "That's not our problem"? How should we think about national boundaries when it comes to water?

Runoff Pollution

Runoff pollution is toxic liquid flowing from the land into waterways from septic tanks, cars, trucks, boats, farms, ranches, and freshwater areas. This waste often makes river, lake, and ocean water unsafe for humans and wildlife.

In the United States, more than one-third of the waters are adverse-ly affected by coastal pollution. In some areas, runoff pollution is so bad that beaches need to be closed following rainstorms. Drinking water supplies can be contaminated by polluted runoff liquid, as can coastal waters containing valuable fish populations. Experts think there is a link between agricultural runoff and waterborne organisms that cause lesions and death in fish. Humans who come in contact with these polluted waters and infected fish can also experience harmful symptoms, such as intestinal illnesses and lead poisoning.

Millions of car and truck engines make miniature "oil spills" every day onto roads and parking lots, which add significantly to runoff pollution. Some water pollution actually starts as air pollution, which settles into waterways and oceans. In addition, topsoil or silt from fields or construction sites can trickle into waterways, harming fish and wildlife habitats.

Correcting the harmful effects of runoff pollution is costly. Each year millions of dollars are spent to restore and protect areas damaged or endangered by these pollutants.

- Well-fertilized lawns may be contributing to fertilizer runoff pollution in your area. When you mow your own or your neighbors' lawns, let the lawn fertilize itself (or "self-mulch") by leaving grass clippings on the ground instead of raking them off.
- A lot of agricultural runoff pollution comes from farms growing grain crops to feed the livestock that provides your hamburger or steak dinner. Could you give up one meat dinner a week? It would help cut down on the need for these grain crops . . . and it's good for you!
- The EPA estimates that "every three weeks, more oil is deposited on driveways and streets in the United States than the Exxon Valdez Oil spill in Alaska." Advise your family to keep cars in good running order even small oil leaks should be fixed quickly.

TEENS IN ACTION

Gishwati, Rwanda
Bamboo Buffers

Students in Rwanda addressed runoff pollution. The Rwanda University Club for Conservation of Biodiversity created a buffer zone in the Gishwati Forest Reserve in the Western province of Rwanda, in connection with the Gishwati Area Conservation Program. They planted bamboo trees in the buffer zone to separate human activities such as agriculture and farming from the Gishwati Forest Reserve and prevent runoff pollution. During this experience, students learned about the importance of reversing environmental damage by planting vegetation to counterbalance the negative effects of human activity.

" We all live upstream from one another. No matter where you live, your actions affect our world's oceans and waterways. **"**
—Philippe Cousteau

Coral Reefs in Crisis

One of the most visible and troubling effects of human treatment of the oceans can be seen in coral reefs, one of the ocean's most prized inhabitants. The amazing hues, intricate shapes, and thousands of fish make healthy coral reefs spectacular underwater places to visit. They are the most biologically diverse areas in the world, more diverse even than rainforests. And each reef is completely unique in its form and the kinds of animals it hosts. A large number of plants and animals that live in coral reefs have not been studied or even named yet. Some of the ones we are studying now—and have yet to study—may give us new medicines to treat cancer, antibiotics to fight infections, or protection from harmful solar rays.

Coral reefs may resemble a sort of plant life, but they are actually formed by coral polyps, which are tiny animals that live in colonies. Each coral polyp builds a little shell, or apartment, for itself out of limestone. Together, the coral polyp colony builds an entire neighborhood of stony apartments stacked on top of one another. Every generation of coral polyp builds a new layer of limestone on top of the last. The nooks and crannies in this intricate neighborhood provide places for other animals such as all types of fish, sponges, sea stars, anemones, turtles, mollusks, crustaceans, snails, sea snakes, and plants to live and visit.

Six major physical factors affect coral reef development:

1. Water temperature

2. Water depth

3. Amount of sunlight penetrating the water

4. Water salinity (saltiness)

5. Amount of sediment in the water

6. Emergence into air (reefs do not like to be exposed to air)

As our ocean water changes, these factors change, causing coral reefs to suffer and sometimes disappear altogether. The main culprits threatening coral reefs are global warming, ocean acidification, erosion, pollution, fishing, and tourism.

Count how many colors you see in this photo.

Now, imagine this reef just all white. Colorless.

"One way to open your eyes is to ask yourself, 'What if I had never seen this before? What if I knew I would never see it again?'"—Rachel Carson, environmentalist and author of *Silent Spring*

Global Warming

As carbon pollution and global warming cause ocean water to heat up to higher than normal temperatures, coral reefs are becoming bleached. All the beautiful colors? Gone. The algae that live inside the coral polyps in a reef are what give coral reefs their brilliant colors. As the water warms, this algae can die off, causing an entire reef to turn white, or "bleach." A few days after bleaching, the coral reef will darken and die. While some corals can survive warmer temperatures, many can't, so slowing the warming of our ocean is of vital importance.

Ocean Acidification

A more acidic ocean affects the mineral called carbonate that the shellfish and corals use to create their shells. Increasing acidification slows the growth of the carbonate and weakens the corals' shells. If pH levels drop enough, the shells will literally dissolve, leaving behind no skeletons, which means no reef.

Erosion and Pollution

During the erosion process, silt, mud, fertilizers, and herbicides that wash off the surrounding land into the sea damage delicate coral reefs. The silt and mud cover the corals in a haze. Fertilizers and untreated sewage release an excess of nutrients into the water, causing certain types of algae to explode in growth, choking the reefs. In addition, oil spills in the ocean suffocate living corals and poison the water around them. It can take many years for a reef community to recover from the damage of a single oil spill.

Fishing and Tourism

Humans, and particularly the fishing and tourism industries, have done a great deal of damage to coral reefs around the world. Factory-fishing vessels that trawl the seafloor often bulldoze right over reefs, destroying an entire underwater neighborhood in a single blow. To attract cruise ships, some coastal communities have literally blasted through the reefs to create boat channels. Divers and snorkelers damage or break fragile coral branches by simply touching them or grazing them with a careless hand or flipper. Dive boat operators and fishers destroy reefs with anchors and propeller blades. Souvenir-seeking tourists snag pieces of coral, which took the reef years to build, and may disrupt the delicate reef ecosystem.

What Can Be Done to Save Our Reefs?

Here are four primary ways people can help:

1. Help stop climate change and ocean acidification by reducing CO_2 emissions. This means using more efficient cars such as hybrids and using responsible wind, solar, and hydro (water) energy wherever possible.

2. Identify a local issue where restoration could have significant outcomes, for example, to reduce erosion, replenish plants and animals, or support fragile environments.

3. Lobby to create protected areas in the ocean known as marine sanctuaries. Examples of marine sanctuaries include the Monterey Bay National Marine Sanctuary in the United States, the Saguenay–St. Lawrence Marine Park in Canada, and the Galápagos Marine Reserve in Ecuador.

4. Campaign to improve fishing practices so that nets do not drag along the bottom of the ocean and destroy the fragile coral reefs and put up signs to inform people about and encourage them to stop such harmful practices.

Is your family planning a vacation? Talk to your parents about choosing eco-friendly lodging and tour operators. Visit ecotourism. org for more information.

mural on a building in St. Thomas, US Virgin Islands **photo credit: Darsi Dreyer**

YOUR TURN

A Slogan for the Waters

Many parts of the world depend on tourism for local livelihood. Yet tourists can sometimes be careless and are often oblivious contributors to water-related problems. What risks or threats does tourism present in your community? Start a campaign to raise awareness of the need to respect our waters and shorelines. Many national parks and forests have slogans like "Leave No Trace" and "Take Only Pictures, Leave Only Footprints" to remind visitors of the care needed to preserve natural areas. What's your slogan to protect a waterway that matters to you? Be creative. Get the word out—use your voice!

TEENS IN ACTION

Tavernier, Florida, United States
Operation Coral Restoration

Coral Shores High School marine science teacher David Makepeace beams as his students explain their coral restoration efforts. "If we don't help the coral out now, they could be gone in our lifetime," says Zach Pardo, a senior who plans to study marine biology. "Do you know there are more than 3,500 corals in the nursery now, and we helped with most of them?" asks senior Jenna Regelmann.

The coral restoration nursery, set up and managed by Coral Restoration Foundation (CRF), is in thirty feet of water more than three miles offshore in the Florida Keys. Since 2003, Coral Shores students have assisted at CRF's coral nursery and various restoration sites around the Upper Keys. Some students lead volunteer groups and make presentations for conferences and civic organizations. Despite the time commitment and physical demand, they can't seem to get enough of the coral restoration work. "Field science, especially underwater, is a lot more glamorous on TV than in real life," observes Makepeace. "The work can be exhausting but the lure of this good work usually results in more kids signing up than the twelve-passenger boat will carry. I'll admit the idea of SCUBA diving during school time is enticing as well."

Senior Dannon Magrane explains: "Our marine studies class has our own coral transplanting site. We mount, clean, and transplant the corals. Transplanting corals means removing corals from propagation modules and relocating them to a coral reef where they can grow. We dive into the water and meet with our groups down on the nursery site. Each group has a propagation module and transplanting discs. We affix the discs onto the module while we wait for our coral cuttings. Then we affix the corals to the disc on a smooth point on the reef. We keep records of every transplanted coral. Then, we grab our cleaning tools and clean older corals by scraping algae off the discs. Certain types of algae prevent the coral from growing and that is why cleaning the coral is so important. Everything we do is to save the coral. I can come back in years to come and see how they have grown."

Coral Shores High School students measure new coral growth. photo credit: David Makepeace

The students also restore seagrass, monitor reef growth, and conduct fish counts. They even venture into advocacy. They have addressed state officials about the importance of maintaining the Florida Keys National Marine Sanctuary. And when they grew troubled by widespread algae blooms in Florida Bay, they spoke to the South Florida Water Management District Governing Board about the need for continued restoration in the Everglades, which affect the algae blooms.

"**For as long as I can remember, my father has been telling me what a beautiful place the Keys was when he was a kid and how it has changed. In my eighteen years, I have seen a decline. I want to try to preserve as much as possible of what is left.**"

—*Malley Burmaster, age 18*

Sensitive Seagrass

Seagrass is a shallow saltwater plant. It's similar to coral reefs because it, too, provides shelter, food, and water purification. Young fish, turtles, anemones, and other ocean animals use seagrass beds as places to live, eat, and hide from predators. Seagrass is very susceptible to the changes in its environment because it needs light more than any other plant in the world. Seagrass sensitivity and reactions inform scientists of ocean changes and may help them predict future ocean trends.

photo credit: NOAA

Seagrass meadows are vital to healthy water and a healthy planet; however, seagrass around the world is disappearing. In fact, nearly half the seagrass in the Mediterranean is gone. Philippe's team at EarthEcho International has been working alongside scientists and young people to support seagrass restoration in Golfo Aranci in Sardinia. Students are helping monitor water quality in the area where seagrass beds are being restored and even growing some seagrass in their classrooms. Using a QR code attached to the plants, scientists can track the growth of the seagrass and share images with students.

YOUR TURN

Be a Change Agent

This book is all about change—how the planet is changing due to global warming and ocean acidification, how weather patterns and food webs change, and most importantly, how young people become agents of *good* change. Find a story of someone who already has taken action in your community to improve the environment. What was the motivation? How did the community respond? What lessons were learned? Knowing the history of change in your community can be helpful in developing your own action plans. History *matters*—as you will see in the next section.

Looking Back: Historical Moments & Actions

What can history tell us about our oceans? How have humans helped and harmed our waterways in the past? Read about some of the champions and significant events that have shaped our water world today.

A Brief History of Ocean Exploration

Early Explorers

The earliest sea explorers rarely ventured out of sight of land. The Polynesians and Phoenicians were first to develop open sea routes. The Polynesians used sophisticated celestial observation to travel among the islands of the South Pacific. Historians believe the Phoenicians sailed from the Mediterranean Sea to the shores of present-day England by 600 BCE. As boats grew sturdier, seafarers ventured farther from home, creating maps that detailed water currents and physical land features.

LEGENDS OF THE SEA

Ancient Greek legends and myths acknowledge the bond between human fortune and the sea. In one famous story, Polykrates, a wealthy builder, casts his most precious object into the sea to avoid the wrath of the gods who might be jealous of his good fortune. But the ring he throws away returns to him in the belly of a fish! Folklore also reveals a deep bond between dolphins and people. Ancient Greeks believed that dolphins loved music and helped fishers. There are countless tales of children being saved by dolphins. In one account, a dolphin carried a child to school every day. When the child died and stopped coming back to the sea, the dolphin perished out of sorrow.

The sea was also feared, due to the frequency of shipwrecks. The sea's often overwhelming power was embodied by the wrathful "earth-shaker" Greek god Poseidon. Historical stories of traversing the sea, like that of Homer's The Odyssey, are filled with accounts of monsters, beasts, and fatal temptations. Even when the sea is considered a playground of fantastical and destructive forces, it proves a resource for the imagination.

The Middle Ages

In Europe, the Vikings made significant explorations during the Middle Ages, establishing trade routes throughout Britain, Ireland, Southern Europe, North Africa, and Central Asia. In the ninth century, a global warming event freed the North Atlantic of ice, allowing the Vikings to travel to Iceland, Greenland, and North America.

About two hundred years later, Chinese explorers invented the magnetic compass, an important navigational tool still used today. Shipbuilding was also well established in China during the Middle Ages. Chinese ships from this time had central rudders and watertight compartments, which can be found in modern ships today. In the late 1300s and early 1400s, Chinese admiral and diplomat Zheng He sailed to countries bordering the Indian Ocean, including Vietnam, Thailand, Malacca, Java, and Sri Lanka. He also sailed to Saudi Arabia, the eastern coast of Africa, Southeast Asia, and India, establishing important trade routes for China. The great medieval Muslim explorer Ibn Battuta traveled extensively to Muslim countries including Saudi Arabia, North Africa, Egypt, Palestine, and Syria, and as far as China and Indonesia, in a series of journeys spanning nearly thirty years. He recorded his travels in his famous rihla, which means "journey" in Arabic.

The Age of Discovery

Europe's Age of Discovery is often attributed to Prince Henry of Portugal, also known as Henry the Navigator. During the 1400s, his devotion to exploring led to mapping the coast of Western Africa, which resulted in valuable trade routes around the Cape of Good Hope and into the Indian Ocean. Then in 1492, an explorer named Christopher Columbus traveled west to the Americas, using the charts built by his predecessors. With accumulated data about coastal topography, winds, waves, and currents, Ferdinand Magellan sailed a full circle around Earth in 1520. Before and during these travels by Europeans, native peoples throughout the Americas and the Arctic explored offshore as well, pioneering elaborate coastal trade networks and making efficient use of abundant marine resources.

Into the Deep

In the mid 1500s, interest in what was below the waves swept through Europe. With crude helmets and diving bells (airtight chambers), early explorers could spend short periods of time underwater. These devices allowed humans to glimpse at plants and fish that were not visible from the surface. Scientists quickly realized that a lot more was going on down there than anybody knew. Continued advances were made with submersible boats able to dive twelve feet below sea level, assisted by air hoses attached to floats at the surface.

Oceanography Comes of Age

During the twentieth century, ship technology changed dramatically. Wartime antisubmarine systems spurred the development of sonar devices, which used underwater sound waves to detect enemy ships. These wartime systems were later refined to assist in the mapping of the deep ocean and the sea floor, and allowed scientists to research and photograph shipwrecks, such as the *Titanic*.

Today, remote-controlled robotic vehicles can go where humans cannot and collect data and samples in trenches that are miles beneath the ocean's surface.

The excitement of ocean exploration is ongoing because there's so much left to discover!

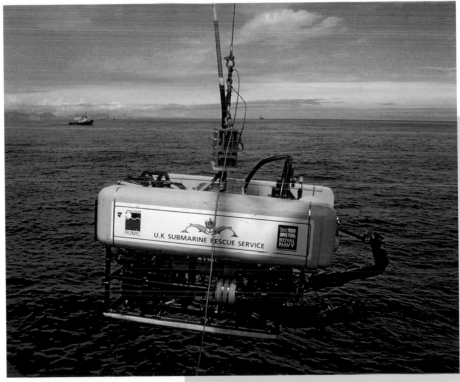

a British Scorpio underwater robot
photo credit: © Handout/British Ministry of Defence/Jonathan Holloway/Reuters/Corbis

Captain Jacques Cousteau: Adventurer, Visionary, and Steward

> "The best way to observe a fish is to become a fish."
>
> —Jacques Cousteau

photo credit: © Bettmann/Corbis

For millennia, explorers traveled the earth's oceans in search of new lands, unfamiliar cultures, and exotic forms of life. Jacques Cousteau, born in southwest France, spent his life traveling these same seas, not in search of the life on its surface, but to discover what lay beneath. His groundbreaking work taught the world that the oceans are vital to our existence, that "water and life are indissolubly bound." He revealed the mystery and majesty of these underwater worlds by building bridges to take us there. In 1943, Cousteau and the engineer Émile Gagnan invented the Aqualung, a wearable oxygen tank (later to become known as SCUBA gear), which allowed for easier and safer diving. He outfitted his boat, the *Calypso,* with his own innovative technologies like the diving saucer and underwater cameras.

With more than sixteen books and films admired by the public and critics alike, Cousteau won three Academy Awards for the documentaries *The Silent World* (1957), *Le Poisson Rouge* (1959), and *World Without Sun* (1965). These films showed the world that rather than fearing the sea and its creatures, like sharks and whales, we must celebrate this thriving ecosystem. He was the first filmmaker to capture the exuberant experience of scuba diving.

Cousteau's visionary project opened up new worlds for countless future explorations, bringing underwater sights to us all. He hoped that understanding and valuing our intimate connection with the ocean would foster a more caring relationship and inspire innovation, such as harnessing the ocean's tides and temperatures to solve Earth's energy crisis. He imagined the day when humans would cultivate their food on the sea floor and was the first person to create an underwater human settlement.

Jacques Cousteau was one of the twentieth century's greatest adventurers. He united his love of technology and exploration in revolutionary ways to teach people about their intimate connection to the bodies of water covering the earth's surface. His dream: that we will all continue to care for our oceans as the tremendous source of life that this Water Planet truly is.

Do you love the underwater world? Get closer to it by swimming with goggles and a snorkel. If you want to try diving, look for a SCUBA certification class near you. Often, you will first train in a swimming pool and then graduate to a lake or coastal area.

SCUBA = Self **C**ontained **U**nderwater **B**reathing **A**pparatus

Jacques Cousteau demonstrates his latest invention, the Aqualung. October 1950.

Dr. Sylvia Earle: Legendary Oceanographer

"Many of us ask what can
I, as one person, do, but
history shows us that
everything good and bad
starts because somebody
does something or does not
do something."—Sylvia Earle

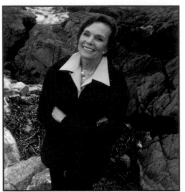

photo credit: © Macduff Everton/Corbis

Like Jacques Cousteau, ocean expert Sylvia Earle was not born along an ocean coast. Instead, she grew up on a New Jersey farm, and came to love nature, wilderness, and exploring. These interests combined to form her life's work: exploring and protecting "the blue heart of the planet"—our waters. The first in her family to go to college, Sylvia studied botany, which she believed was necessary to understanding ecosystems, and earned her degree in 1955.

While attending university, Sylvia learned to SCUBA dive. This was a critical step that led her to participate in numerous research projects all over the world. In 1969, she led the first team of women **aquanauts** to live in an underwater research station off the coast of the Virgin Islands for two weeks. Dive after dive, Sylvia has provided research that has helped people understand the ocean floors, the impact of human conflicts and wars on oceans, and the need for marine animal protection. She has spent more than seven thousand hours conducting research underwater, and continues as an explorer today. Sylvia Earle transformed her childhood love of the outdoors originating on her family farm into a true spirit of discovery that benefits humans everywhere.

An **aquanaut** (similar to a "water astronaut") is a scuba diver who remains in an underwater habitat on the seafloor conducting research for an extended time period, usually twenty-four or more continuous hours.

Animal Lifeguards

Archie Carr: The Turtle Guy

Archie Carr protected turtles. A zoologist, ecologist, and conservationist, his work extended to many animal species, yet his dedicated efforts to understand and document the lives of sea turtles charted new territory. Growing up in Savannah, Georgia, Archie had a backyard filled with cages of snakes, lizards, and turtles. Yet it was in the coastal areas of the Caribbean, the Americas, east Africa, and Australia that Archie tracked sea turtle migration and navigation. He took a firm stand against commercial sea turtle "ranching" and the removal of sea turtles from the endangered species list. From 1959 to 1968, he led Operation Green Turtle, which distributed turtle eggs and hatchlings to protected beaches, to save turtle populations from the brink of extinction. Archie made a tremendous influence through his studies, his activism, his teaching, and his tireless efforts to establish places where turtles still thrive today.

"For most of the wild things on Earth, the future must depend upon the conscience of [hu]mankind."

—Archie Carr

Jasmin Graham: Shark Scientist

Jasmin Graham describes her work as a combination of conservation, shark science, communication, and social justice. She specializes in elasmobranch (sharks, rays, skates, and sawfish) ecology and evolution. Beyond her work researching sharks, Jasmin is passionate about science education and making shark and marine sciences accessible for underrepresented minority students. In 2020, she cofounded MISS (Minorities in Shark Sciences) with Black female shark researchers Amani Webber-Schultz, Carlee Jackson, and Jaida Elcock. They strive to promote diversity and inclusion in shark science and encourage gender minorities of color to contribute knowledge to marine science.

Making History Today: Movers & Shakers

We tend to think about history as only in the past. However, history is actually in the making at every moment. So who are today's history makers?

Alexandra Cousteau: Modern Explorer and Cofounder of Oceans2050

Alexandra Cousteau, grand-daughter of Jacques Cousteau and sister of Philippe Cousteau, is an award-winning advocate for ocean restoration and abundance. A leading figure in ocean activism, Alexandra collaborates with world leaders to influence, organize, and mobilize action to make the oceans more biodiverse and abundant. As cofounder of Oceans2050, Alexandra combines her gift for storytelling and background in political science to bring people

photo credit: OCEANS2050

together around the common goal of restoring the ocean's abundance.

In addition to her work with Oceans2050, Alexandra has also led numerous expeditions around the world. In 2010, as an "emerging explorer" for National Geographic, Alexandra joined others in redefining what exploration means in the twenty-first century. With most of our planet's land already observed, traversed, and inventoried, how can this term be defined for a new era and remain meaningful, new, and exciting? According to Alexandra, today an explorer might "explore an issue or see a place through new eyes. While there are not many places I can go for the first time, I can explore them through new ideas and parameters, and with new and innovative tools."

The purpose of modern exploration has a new dimension—inspiring people to take care of and work to restore the places we already know. For Alexandra, this involves viewing our environment through a specific lens: the water cycle. "From the top of Mount Everest to the deepest oceans and all the way around," she explains, "we live within a continuous flow of water. The water from the Ganges in India could rain over the plains of Kenya, end up in a cup of tea in the Queen's castle, or fill a swimming pool in a Dallas suburb. When we know this, we may behave differently and take action in our own lives."

What does a modern explorer's life entail? Alexandra says, "Every day is different. Some days I curl up on my couch reading and doing research. I might be at an airport traveling to a speaking engagement. Sometimes I start early with my film crew on an expedition investigating human and natural elements of water. We work to tell the story of our water planet. We aim to shape society's dialogue to include water as one of the defining issues of our century by illustrating the interconnectedness of all water issues. We may have challenges and stress as well as moments of elation and triumph. But while not always easy, the work is always exciting. Our work is meant to add to our global conversation about important matters in a way that leads people toward action."

Explore with Alexandra two spectacular water systems:

THE MANDATORY MEKONG

"In Cambodia we traveled the Mekong River to the Tonle Sap Lake, the largest lake in Southeast Asia. Every year in May, the river flow reverses because the Mekong cannot absorb all the water. Over three months, the lake floods and the entire area transforms. To adapt, people live in floating communities. There are entire villages with homes on platforms, and churches and fuel stations all on boats! People travel from place to place by boat. The surrounding forests flood to the treetops. The birds and cats and otters move to dry areas at the tops of trees. With the forest floods, the fish have lots of food from drowning insects. All fish are spawning during this

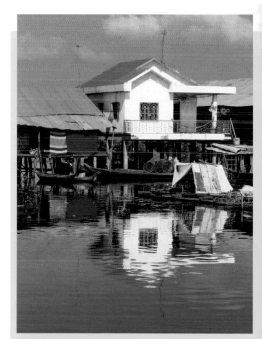

a modern and an old house on the Mekong River near Battambang, Cambodia time, and the baby fish can hide in the branches of trees. When the dry season comes, the lake recedes, and these now larger fish move down the Mekong—in a 'direct delivery' food system to support people all along the river. As industry starts to build dams on the Mekong, one of the largest inland food ecosystems in the world will be disrupted. Along this river and lake, everyone depends on hundreds of fish species unique to Cambodia. These people function with and rely on nature."

> **"If there is magic on this planet, it is contained in water. It is life."**
> —Alexandra Cousteau, explorer

THE MIGHTY MISSISSIPPI

In the United States, the Mississippi River attracts Alexandra's explorer's eye, especially since this 2,340-mile river and its tributaries reach thirty-one states and two Canadian provinces. "The Mississippi, or Huck Finn's river, has importance historically, culturally, industrially, and agriculturally, and supports human, animal, and plant life as it flows to the Gulf of Mexico. And *all* is threatened. Pollution caused by farms—in Minnesota, Iowa, Tennessee, and Arkansas, to name a few—from over-fertilization and waste from other industries dumps excessive nutrients into the Mississippi. A quart of motor oil carelessly tossed down a drain in Montana, Pennsylvania, or Missouri joins with all the other garbage to create a dead zone in the Gulf of Mexico the size of New Jersey—about seven thousand square miles. Shrimp are jumping out of the water onto the beaches trying to breathe due to **eutrophication.** The fishers who depend on the region can't make a living anymore. We have to reverse this through deliberate actions."

> **Eutrophication** is a concentration of chemicals that increases the growth of plankton and depletes the water of oxygen, which harms dependant life forms.

Alexandra observes, "In both of these locales, we depend on rivers and their tributaries for our health and well-being. Our actions can either make these resources scarce or incapable of supporting life, *or* they can reflect that our lives depend on water."

So You Want to Be an Explorer?
Start by exploring your own watershed. Canoe around it. Hike through it. Explore it with a camera, write your observations in a journal, or create a video or audio recording. Make podcasts. Map your watershed, take photos, and post the images online. Talk about what you see and what changes you think need to be made. Bring what you see to the attention of your school, local officials, and community representatives. Use the information you discover to inspire people to explore and take action. Become a community leader and role model.

Greta Thunberg: Climate Change Activist

You've probably heard of Greta Thunberg, the young environmental activist from Sweden. She is best known for challenging world leaders to take action on climate change. Greta began learning about climate change when she was eight years old, and in 2018, when she was fifteen, Thunberg took action.

SCHOOL STRIKE FOR CLIMATE ———————

Inspired by students in Florida who were walking out of school to protest gun violence, Greta began spending her school days outside the Swedish center of government. During these protests, she held a sign reading "School strike for climate." This simple act of resistance was soon noticed by the media. And like a stone dropped into water, it caused ripples. Greta's strike inspired teens all over the world to organize their own school climate strikes as part of the Fridays for Future movement. And in 2019, activists from all over the world collaborated to coordinate the first Global Strike for Climate, which had over 1.6 million participants in 125 countries.

While there's still much work to do in mitigating climate change, Greta's story is an example of the power a single person has to inspire others to create change.

> "When I'm taking action, I don't feel like I am helpless and that things are hopeless, because then I feel like I'm doing everything I can."
>
> —Greta Thunberg

Alex Lin: Modern Innovator

"In fifth grade I was part of a school community problem-solving program, and we wanted to find an issue that mattered," said Alex Lin. "In 2004, I brought in a newspaper article about the e-waste (electronic waste) problem, which became larger than a one-year project. We chose this topic for the WIN Team—Westerly Innovations Network—formed by me and some of my friends."

Alex explains the process his WIN Team followed:

"We read about the national e-waste issue and began conducting research to see the local need and what was already being done. We did surveys and interviews with local recycling companies; these came in handy when it came time to set up the recycling program. We approached the city council and there was no method for recycling e-waste. Then a WIN Team member's neighbor was going to dump about fifty computers in the trash. This large-scale situation propelled us into action to make a sustainable plan. We sought to show our town a model system that could be replicated in other areas."

The WIN Team established three priorities: **Recycle, Refurbish,** and **Legislate.**

RECYCLE

"We realized we needed sustainability that would come from a recycling receptacle in the town—a permanent transfer station that reliably disposes of electronics," said Lin. "When someone gets a new computer, usually they throw the old one away. When computers are discarded in landfills, the lead, cadmium, and other heavy minerals soak into the groundwater. We installed a receptacle at the transfer station that was provided by a local company that recycles electronics. This is an example of how partnerships are key to creating sustainable systems.

"Education is crucial. Many people don't know about the e-waste problem. At the beginning, based on our surveys, only about 13 percent of the local populace knew about proper disposal. Now it's about 100 percent. We presented to all the local elementary schools and gave them flyers and surveys to get back to us. We even had a lottery for returned surveys—the winner received a refurbished computer!

We spoke to high schools and community groups, and we wrote articles for newspapers about how people can get involved.

"We have now recycled over 300,000 pounds of electronic waste—an average of between 2,000 and 5,000 pounds a month."

REFURBISH

"Refurbishing (repairing and reusing) electronics is about seven times more efficient than recycling because of the energy and resource consumption associated with recycling. Our efforts resulted in the refurbishing of over three hundred computers to give to students. Who helped? Other students! We worked with our school's computer repair class and integrated computer refurbishing into their curriculum. The donated computers came from companies, banks, and individuals and went to local residents. Then we set our sights on distant places where young people lack electronic technology. We have WIN Children's Centers with computers in Sri Lanka, Mexico, Cameroon, and the Philippines—in places that need electronic technology."

Do you know a young person who is making a difference in the world? Nominate them for a Brower Youth Award at broweryouthawards.org.

LEGISLATE

"How did we legislate? At first we did more research to know our materials inside and out, and also to learn about various electronics bills already created in other states. We met with local legislators because there was one such bill proposed in Rhode Island. We asked a lot of questions. We pushed for the bill, even testified. But the result was it did not pass.

"We regrouped and considered: Why didn't it pass? The language was too complicated. So I took the bill, simplified the wording into a resolution that we would propose to our town, get it passed there, and then expand it to the state level. The resolution was simple: Ban the dumping of electronic waste. Clear and concise. The town council of 2005 unanimously passed our proposal! No one in Westerly could dump their electronics. Then our representative, Peter Lewis, took it to the state. We collected signatures for petitions to influence politicians. We testified before the environment committee. We gave a detailed presentation that was well received. We showed what twelve- and thirteen-year-old kids can do!"

In 2006, the State of Rhode Island passed a bill that banned the improper disposal of e-waste. The WIN Team was instrumental in helping pass the bill. The law went into place in July 2007.

Advice from Alex and the WIN Team

1. Make your plans and system sustainable.

2. Define the need.

3. Research and find partners.

4. Target your actions to where they are most useful.

5. Find the best solution with the greatest impact.

Remember: Being a young person usually works in your favor!

"We were determined. We would have testified again and again. In a certain way, kids have an almost louder voice than adults. When you find a topic you care about, do the hard work, and find your voice, people will listen. Our voices are powerful."

Is Alex's work done? Not a chance. He is now influencing a new generation of changemakers through his organization Eco Geek, which aims to inspire teen environmental activism. Visit his website ecogeek.weebly.com.

time for REFLECTION

Read this section again and think about how many careers are mentioned—from ocean explorer to politician to news reporter. Any career can have a connection to saving our oceans and waterways. What career do you have in mind? In what ways could you help our planet while in this profession?

SUMMARY

Preparation. In arming yourself with knowledge of the planet's interconnected water systems, you have prepared for action. You have chosen the need you want to address and learned a lot of background information about it—including possible causes and solutions, what's been done in the past to meet this need, and what is being done today. Preparation extends beyond investigation by giving you the "big picture" of how every water issue you address affects every other, and the larger history and facts surrounding all these issues.

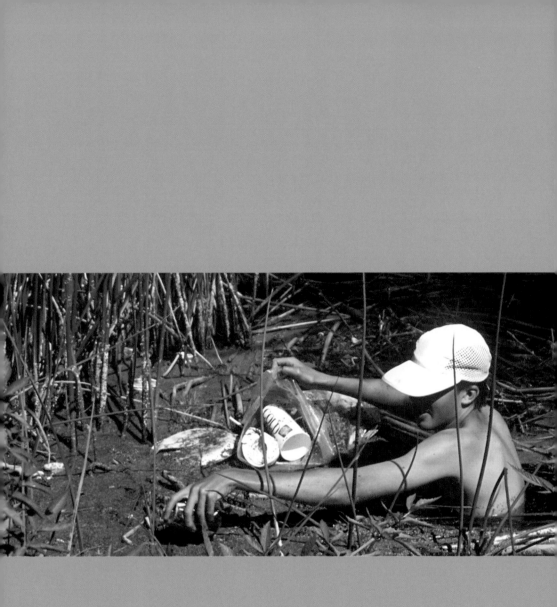

STAGE 3
GET GOING→ACT

Knowledge prepares us and begins to generate ideas. Examples of what other young people have done help us start considering the planning process. All of this comes together as we move into stage 3: *taking action to save our waters.*

The Story of Tar Creek: Part 3

Miami, Oklahoma, United States

How Did They Act?

The students published their research papers, poetry, and personal essays in two anthologies that tell their story, and they gave "toxic tours" to hundreds of other students and adults from the region to educate them about the Tar Creek Superfund site. They put up signs to keep kids out of the water and off the mounds of toxic dirt where they used to ride bikes. The students also hosted an annual conference that brought together state and national government officials, leaders of Native groups, and members of the surrounding community to wrestle with the environmental and personal issues that resulted from the pollution.

The Story of Tar Creek continues on page 132.

Your Little Choices Make a Big Splash

It's true: your daily choices and actions make all the difference to our planet's water system, whether or not you intend them to. Even your choices about things that may seem—on the surface—unrelated to water.

Our lifestyles include cars, fast food, disposable items (including paper plates and plastic sandwich bags), newspapers, air conditioning, cell phones, household appliances (such as microwaves and hairdryers), and many other items (including single-use masks and gloves) that make our lives safer, easier, and more comfortable. Unfortunately, pollution is often a consequence of producing, using, and disposing of these items. Waste is unwanted or discarded material. When waste is not contained, it is released into the environment and becomes pollution. Pollution generated by industries, agriculture, businesses, schools, vehicles, and even our homes, if not properly handled, can contaminate our soil, water, and air. Once pollution is generated, it is pretty much here to stay. Even if it is eventually contained, pollution can meanwhile seep permanently into the earth's landscape, including our oceans and waterways.

When you plan your course of action, consider the following topics and the inspiring ways kids around the world are tackling them.

> **❝ Everything you do makes a difference. ❞**
> —Philippe Cousteau

Be a Conscious Consumer

The next time you go to the store, think carefully about what you buy. Consumerism, or purchasing more than we need, is a huge issue impacting our waterways today and in the future.

Consider your cotton T-shirt, for example. Water is needed to grow the cotton for the fabric. Water is needed in the manufacturing process, and it's needed to transport your shirt (often across oceans and continents) to your local store. All in all, it takes about 713 gallons of water, plus a lot of energy, to get your T-shirt from the cotton fields to your home.

Bright colors and prints might catch your eye, but textile dyeing is the second largest polluter of clean water, after agriculture. And what happens once you outgrow the shirt or stop wearing it? If you throw it away in the trash, it can end up in a landfill or as pollution.

That's a pretty big water cost for one little shirt. Now consider this: *every* product you buy has a water cost. When you think about it this way, you can begin to see how the decisions you make have an impact on water—from the clothes and products you buy to the foods you eat to the transportation choices you make. It's all connected.

But there's good news! By making more environmentally friendly choices, such as purchasing clothes and other products made from eco-friendly materials like hemp and bamboo, eating more plant-based meals, recycling and thrifting, and just buying less in general, you can do your part to save water and the planet.

Need the scoop on what and how to recycle? Check out earth911.com for facts and resources. Or go straight to wireflytradeins.cexchange.com to turn in your old smartphones, game consoles, and electronics for cash or donations to your favorite nonprofit organizations (including EarthEcho International!).

Electronics Recycling

Electronics are an integral part of our daily lives. Even in remote areas, people stay connected via smartphones, using solar chargers to reenergize batteries in places where there is no electricity. Electronic waste, or e-waste, accounts for *70 percent* of the toxic waste currently found in landfills in the United States. In addition to valuable metals like aluminum, electronics often contain hazardous materials like mercury, lead, or Freon. When placed in a landfill, even small amounts of these materials can contaminate soil and drinking water. It is critical that these items—including smartphones, computers, televisions, batteries, air conditioners, microwaves, and others—be disposed of properly.

On page 102, you read about Alex Lin and his WIN Team's efforts to prevent e-waste, by recycling or refurbishing old computers and making it illegal for people to improperly dispose of their electronics. However, it also matters which electronics we choose to buy in the first place. With pressure from consumer groups, some manufacturers are starting to offer products intentionally designed to be easily disassembled so they can be easily refurbished and safely recycled.

Farming & Food

You probably have figured out by now that all Earth's ecosystems are interrelated. A straw that accidentally slips out of a person's hand in Idaho can end up along a beach in Mexico. Melting glaciers in the Arctic Circle can influence the rainy season in Bangladesh. And what you choose to eat for breakfast, lunch, and dinner has an effect on what a person in Kenya eats for breakfast, lunch, and dinner . . . or rather, what they might not have to eat.

TEENS IN ACTION

Minneapolis, Minnesota, United States
Hazardous Chemicals? Not in My Water!

How can families and communities learn about how the products they purchase affect their health and environment? Students in grades 6–8 at the Blake School in Minneapolis decided to teach them. They made an inventory of products in their homes, researched how hazardous the products were depending on their chemical content and their environmental effects if disposed of improperly, and then learned proper disposal methods. Students labeled these products in their homes and presented their research to families and other students in the community. Parents expressed amazement to learn they were using potentially toxic chemicals in their households, even in common cleaning products, and what their effects are on humans and other organisms in the surrounding environment.

The results of the Blake students' efforts? A community of smarter shoppers who know how to make informed decisions when purchasing household items, and also when disposing of them. In the long run, these actions will increase the health of local waterways and send a message to manufacturers that consumers want environmentally friendly products.

What do vinegar, baking soda, lavender, and lemon juice have in common? These and other natural ingredients are used to create household cleansers that are safe and toxin-free. Search the internet for recipes to make your own cleaning products. Remember, what you use in the shower goes down the drain too. Choose shampoo and bath products that are phosphate-free, have low water content or are in bar form, and include minimal or recycled packaging.

Growing food, whether to produce rice for people or feed for livestock, requires vast quantities of water. In the United States alone, agricultural needs are the largest use of fresh water in the world. Every day 145 billion gallons of water is used to irrigate 62 million acres of crop-land. This is three times the amount of water used by US citizens for personal needs. For example, it takes about 400 gallons of water to produce one pound of wheat using current flood irrigation methods. One pound of rice requires about 900 gallons of water. One gallon of ethanol fuel from corn takes about 1,000 gallons of water. And to grow enough cat-tle feed grain to produce just one pound of beef takes about 2,000 gallons of water.

Water runoff from agricultural land pollutes water in streams, rivers, lakes, and the ocean. The most common farming practices create serious water pollution by using vast amounts of synthetic

Composting is the process of using organic waste products to fertilize soil for gardening. You can compost wherever you live, even in an urban setting. Learn the basics at howtocompost.org and start composting at school and at home.

nitrogen-based fertilizers. This has become a major source of nitrous oxide, a greenhouse gas pollutant. And cows—they make enormous quantities of the greenhouse gas methane from their flatulence (you can figure out what that is).

What can farmers do? They can use other methods of farming that prove safer for our environment and the food on our tables. Perennial crops, crop rotation, no-till farming, and manure-based fertilizers can all reduce the pollution and soil erosion caused by farming. And methods like organic agriculture and composting produce fewer byproducts that harm the environment.

Overfishing

Humans are depleting the oceans of fish. Entire species of fish are being targeted and destroyed, disrupting the entire food web and impacting our ocean's ecosystems. For example, after decades of overfishing, the bluefin tuna population in the north Atlantic had declined by 97 percent. This fish became a symbol of the misfortune of many large fish that are hunted until their once-massive numbers become so diminished they are declared endangered. However, due to conservation efforts and more sustainable management practices, bluefin tuna are beginning to make a comeback.

Overfishing happens when the number of fish caught exceeds the number of fish needed to sustain fish populations in a given region. Fishers endanger one species and then turn to another, more plentiful species, thus continuing the decline of food supplies in the ocean. When fishers or consumers desire a particular species of fish, like bluefin tuna, they treat it as if it were unlimited. However, all natural resources, including ocean fish such as the bluefin tuna, are limited. As the human population grows and our demand for fish grows, supply

---

Can a depleted farm be reinvigorated to be filled with vegetables, fruit trees, and a range of livestock—all living together (with humans) in harmony and balance with the natural world? After years of perseverance, patience, and plenty of work, Molly and John Chester call Apricot Lane Farms just that, "a reawakened ecosystem," interdependent and thriving. Their endeavor began in 2011 and has since grown to become a 234-acre organic, biodynamic, and regenerative working farm.

Want to learn more? Watch their award-winning 2018 documentary, The Biggest Little Farm, to see for yourself how this evolution is possible.

simply cannot meet demand. Some scientists estimate that seafood may disappear by 2048 unless something changes.

Too many fishing boats are on the ocean—especially large-scale, industrial vessels such as factory trawlers—with too much capacity for devastating fish populations and seafloor habitats such as coral reefs and sponges. To picture how many fish one factory trawler can catch at one time, imagine a net as large as four football fields. The bottom trawler drags heavy gates and traps across the seafloor, destroying the underwater terrain (including coral reefs), killing marine life as the net gathers every creature in its path, and then discarding the unwanted sea life.

"Imagine using a bulldozer to catch songbirds for food—that's what [bottom trawling] is like. After a trawler has gone by, [the sea floor] looks like a superhighway, it's just flat. Nobody's home. A few fish may swim in and out, but the residents are just smothered, they're crushed. It's like paving them over."—Sylvia Earle, oceanographer

---

factory trawlers fish for pollack in the Bering Sea, Alaska

photo credit: © Natalie Fobes/Science Faction/Corbis

In the long term, overfishing can result in loss of jobs, lost biological diversity, and ecosystem collapse. Sustainable use of our oceans is crucial to human survival. Aquaculture (marine agriculture) may provide an alternative to the depletion of fish in the ocean and might have ecological and economic benefits to fisheries. Most important is saving the supply of fish in the ocean.

Fish Food Facts

- The earliest use of the ocean by humans was probably for food.
- Coastal waters have more productivity than most open-ocean waters and support larger populations of fish.
- Inshore fish populations started to decline in Europe during the 1300s.
- More people + more fishing = the reduction of many ocean fish populations.

Do you like eating fish? That's fine, but if you want to make sure that fish still exist in the future, choose sustainable seafood in restaurants and at your grocery store. The Monterey Bay Aquarium offers recommendations for which options to avoid, which are the best options, and good alternatives in their Seafood Watch guides. Visit seafoodwatch.org to view the guides digitally or download a PDF.

ff Not enough sustainable seafood currently exists in the world to supply the current demand. Not only must we choose sustainable seafood, we must cut our consumption considerably and stop eating and wasting so much of this precious resource. **JJ**
—Philippe Cousteau

Eating Local

Think about what you had for lunch. Did it come with a suitcase and a bus ticket? Actually, it probably did—you just can't see it. In the United States, most food travels about 1,200 miles before it lands on your plate. Pineapples from Hawai'i, oranges from Florida, rice from Texas, maple syrup from Vermont, salmon from Alaska, peppers from Mexico, blueberries from Canada, and broccoli from China. Today most people have no idea where the food on their plate originated, much less how it was grown, even if it's labeled "organic." If you really want to know your food, the best way is to try to eat locally grown products. Whether a product is certified organic or not, any farming that minimizes the use of chemical fertilizers and pesticides is better for us and for our oceans. Many smaller farms that are not certified organic still use organic methods. The best way to know how good a farm's practices are for the planet is to talk to the farmer. Shake the hand that feeds you. Search out a local market or community garden and buy from a local farmer as often as possible.

Talk with your family about shopping at local farmers' markets and buying organic to reduce the use of pesticides. Visit localharvest.org to find farms and farmers' markets near you. Also stop by ewg.org/foodnews to download the Shopper's Guide to Pesticides in Produce—including the top "Dirty Dozen" fruits and veggies that you should try to buy organic, if that's in your budget.

Your Turn: Eat Local

Where, oh where, does your food come from? Find out. Check with the school cafeteria, local grocery store, or a neighborhood restaurant. Are large supermarkets that truck in food the only option for your groceries? Or is there a farmers' market or food co-op near you where farmers sell local produce? Is there a community garden nearby? Maybe you even have space for a garden or a few potted plants where you live. Think of ways you can move the source of what you eat closer to home.

Eating Plant-Based Foods

Another way to go blue in your everyday life is to eat less meat and animal products like eggs and dairy, since these food sources have a much higher water footprint than plant-based options. (Remember, 2,000 gallons—or 7,500 liters—of water are needed to produce one pound of beef.) Not sure how to get started? You might start by eating one plant-based meal a week. Once you've learned some new recipes, you can expand to eat plant-based for one full day each week—breakfast, lunch, and dinner. Encourage your family and friends to join you too. Water-conscious kids worldwide participate in Meatless Mondays to improve their health and the health of the planet.

Take Action

How can you help save our waterways and oceans? Get active. Get involved. Get others to join you. And take action! You have the facts, you have heard the call, and you have plenty of examples to get you inspired. So what will you do? Select one of the following actions or combine several—and get out there.

Choose Your Kind of Action

- **Do It Now!** Get directly involved in recycling, restoring, and protecting.

- **Be a Message Maker.** Is social media your jam? Or do you envision large signs in your neighborhood reminding people to recycle or reuse household items? Communicate! Find creative ways to get out your message using public service announcements, posters, pamphlets, blogs, videos, and that all-important **elevator speech**.

- **Join with Established Groups.** Who in your community would be delighted to have energetic young people helping out, sharing ideas, and getting things accomplished? Work alongside other people who care about the environment and our waters.

- **Raise Funds.** Keep in mind that any way you raise dollars for a charitable pro-ocean cause needs to respect the earth and our environment—and teach others along the way.

- **Walk the Talk.** Be a role model for others by making choices that show you care about our Water Planet.

- **Start a Campaign.** Get out there and campaign for your cause. You might encourage people to turn off electronics that aren't being used and turn them on to riding bikes, which is good for their health *and* good for the environment.

- **Be Political.** The key to creating sustainable change is to become an advocate—especially since our waters and their inhabitants can't speak for themselves. How have other adults and kids made their voices heard? What can young people do locally, nationally, and internationally to instigate necessary change?

  - Find out what your politicians think about and care about, and who on their political staff is responsible for environmental issues and causes.

  - Write letters to public officials when policy is being developed or when a topic deserves their attention.

  - Let your public officials know what you are doing—as you get started, along the way, and as your activities culminate. Invite them to be part of your team.

What's Your Elevator Speech?

Imagine you step into an elevator and the president of your country is there and says, "What's on your mind?" At most, you have about ten seconds per floor as you ride the elevator. That's your "elevator speech." Have one ready!

- Know your key points—what you care about, what needs to happen, what you will do, and what others can do.

- Use short sentences that convey vivid images.

- Make solid eye contact.

- Mean what you say and say what you mean.

Philippe Cousteau's Elevator Speech

1st floor: Did you know that water is the single most important substance on the planet?

2nd floor: Water connects every being to one another—from drinking to energy production.

3rd floor: Water is quickly becoming the cause of the greatest crises of our century.

4th floor: I run a nonprofit called EarthEcho International, and we just launched the Water Planet Challenge.

5th floor: This Challenge empowers teens to bring about global change in our oceans and waterways.

6th floor: With cutting-edge technology, we can reach more than 25 million teens and keep track of the collective impact of all of their environmental projects.

7th floor: Are you ready to help? Here's what you can do . . . (*Hint:* Always have an idea about how the person you're talking to can get involved.)

"We have a stewardship responsibility to maintain healthy, resilient, and sustainable oceans, coasts, and Great Lakes resources for the benefit of this and future generations."—Barack Obama, US President

Holding a Fundraiser?

Make sure the funds you raise for an organization will go toward the cause you seek to support. Read the organization's literature. Do research about how they spend their dollars. Ask what percentages of their funds go directly to the important work that needs to be accomplished.

Who Are Your Political Changemakers?

Know your local, state, or provincial representatives. Attend events where you can meet them and hear them speak. Ask questions about their stances on environmental issues—and on local water issues in particular. Tell them what you and other kids are up to. Keep a log of who is on the "blue" team (pro-oceans and waterways), and remember: you will vote one day!

Read up on the people in your government who care about the environment. Visit League of Conservation Voters (lcv.org) for more information on environmental issues and how representatives in your area have voted in the past.

TEENS IN ACTION

Santa Fe, New Mexico, United States
Fighting Phosphates

Meet Sachiko Cooper DaSilva, a guitar player who knits, skis, and knows her phosphates. At the Santa Fe Girls School in New Mexico, Sachi joined other seventh and eighth graders in studying local water issues. For over seven years, students at the school have been spending time along the Santa Fe River below the wastewater treatment plant. On the nine-acre PRESERVE (which stands for Protecting the River Environment, Stopping Erosion, and Restoring the Vital Ecology), students get their hands dirty removing nonnative Russian olive trees and Siberian elms. In an interview, Sachi explained, "These invasive tree species absorb too much water and push out the native species such as the willows and cottonwoods. We have been lopping and spraying. However, instead of using environmentally harmful chemicals, our spray is made from vinegar and molasses. This slows growth and, after a few times, the spray gets into the roots and the nonnative plant dies."

The students also checked water clarity, total dissolved solids, temperature, and pH, and tested for copper, nitrates, and phosphates. For Sachi, the most important of these elements is phosphates—mineral deposits used as a fertilizer. The EPA phosphate standard for unpolluted water is 0.01 mg/L; just downstream from Santa Fe, the students found phosphate was testing at a whopping 4.25 mg/L. Plants depend on phosphates to grow, but too many can cause eutrophication (chemical nutrient concentration). This leads to oxygen depletion, harms aquatic species, and threatens biodiversity. To make matters worse, decaying debris can build up in streambeds, converting rivers into swamps. Once this happens, there is no water source that people can use.

The class sought to participate in a State Water Commission hearing. Could a group of teenage girls voice their opinions in government and be heard? "We decided to talk about phosphates because we knew about them," Sachi said. "We had presented to our school, knew the data, and even had made a short movie on the topic." The group asked the commission to consider establishing a standard for phosphates in the Santa Fe River. They also asked the commission to support a local ban on the sale of common household and industrial products that contain phosphates, including certain detergents.

On the day of the commission hearing, icy weather closed the schools in Santa Fe . . . and it was Sachi's birthday. "Our parents drove us to the capitol building, the Roundhouse. We walked into the building. Three of us were chosen to speak to the legislators: myself, Maddy, and Moriah. After being sworn in, we sat before the commission. In front of us was the board, plus a stenographer typing every word we spoke, and we testified—to add our voices to the record and influence public policy.

"A lot of kids think we can't change the world right now—but we really tried to change a law that would open eyes in other states as to how bad phosphates are for our environment. Phosphates are found in detergents and fertilizers we use every day. It takes so much money and energy to remove this in the wastewater plants. Instead, stop selling phosphates in products! We can find replacements, and if consumers demand different ingredients, then that's what will be manufactured. Right now, big companies are profiting in a way that hurts our economy and nature. Of course we have other planetary concerns—but remember, phosphates are a cause of eutrophication and that affects the web of life."

The Four Steps to Action

After reading this far, what's on your mind? Which concerns grab you the most? Perhaps a news headline sparked your thinking, or one of these Teens in Action stories stirred up some ideas. Now is the time to really get your action on—and persuade others to join you—by following these four steps:

Step 1: Think about the needs in your community involving water directly, or any related topic that can affect our oceans and waterways.

Step 2: Consider what you know about this subject—both the cause and who is involved in the solution. Align yourself with partners or join people already in the process of improving what needs help.

Step 3: Find out more! Remember the tips on action research (pages 20–21) and use media, interviews, surveys, and your own observation and experience to increase what you know (rehearse your elevator speech!).

Step 4: Put your action plan on paper. List who will do what by when. Keep track of resources you need along the way.

SPREAD THE LOVE!

Get out and enjoy the natural water resources our planet has to offer! Then, encourage others to do the same. People are more likely to protect what they know and love. If you live in the United States, visit one of the National Marine Sanctuaries: sanctuaries.noaa.gov. In Canada, visit Parks Canada: pc.gc.ca, and under "Places," click on "National Marine Conservation Areas." For a worldwide list, visit World Heritage at whc.unesco.org/en/list and filter by "Marine and Coastal" or "Natural." You might also visit an aquarium in your area.

Need More Ideas for Action?
Tackle Trash:

- Pick up litter and dispose of it properly. (Remember: Debris in our waterways doesn't fall from the sky; it falls from our own hands and eventually ends up in our lakes, rivers, and oceans.)
- Take your commitment year-round—join local beach, river, or stream cleanups, even when the weather isn't pleasant.
- Use reusable cloth bags for groceries and shopping instead of disposable plastic bags.
- If you come across a plastic holder for a six-pack of cans or bottles, cut the plastic rings apart and dispose of them properly.
- Use reusable or biodegradable food and beverage containers rather than single-use Styrofoam or plastic containers.
- Reduce, Reuse, Recycle, and Rethink!—and avoid products with excessive packaging and avoid unnecessary purchases.
- Talk "trash" with your friends and family—spread the word about the trashing of our waterways!

> ***Vampire power*** is the wasted use of energy by any electric appliances or gadgets that remain plugged in when not in use. An easy way to reduce vampire power is to connect all your electronics to power strips that can be quickly turned on and off. You can also reduce general electricity waste by using electricity during off-peak hours.

Reduce Pollution:

- Use more efficient energy sources, such as compact fluorescent light bulbs.
- Turn off lights when you leave the room and be sure your electronics are turned off and unplugged.
- Know what goes down the drain. Remind family members to dispose of car oil, engine fluids, cleaners, medicines, or household chemicals in safe ways. Find approved motor oil and household chemical recycling or disposal facilities near your home and tell people about them.

Write a Proposal

To be taken seriously in the world, putting your ideas into a written proposal lets people know that *you mean business.* So make that proposal, make it convincing, and get others involved.

A written proposal also enables you to share your plans with others, whether you are initiating your idea in school, on your own, or with friends. If you need permission to move your plan forward, perhaps from a teacher, principal, community group, or elected official, a proposal will help make it happen. A written document gives legitimacy to your idea when you want to involve people or groups as partners. Be sure to clarify every partner's responsibilities and add them to the proposal. Getting feedback about your proposal often results in buy-in and ongoing support from the readers, so engage people you admire in your process. Often proposals are submitted to funders when money or supplies are needed to get the job done. Learning how to write a formal proposal will open many doors for you as you develop the skills to be a proponent for action.

☑ What goes into your proposal? Here's a checklist of what is typically included—use the categories that match your situation.

☑ Names of people involved

☑ Name of your group or organization

☑ Name of action plan

☑ Community need (Why is this plan necessary?)

☑ Purpose (How will this plan meet the need?)

☑ Partners (Who else—individuals or organizations—will be involved?)

☑ Participation (Who will do what?)

☑ Outcomes (What impact do you expect to happen as a result of your efforts?)

☑ Evidence (How will you track the change being made?)

☑ Resources (What supplies or materials will you need to get the job done?)

☑ Timeline (What will happen when?)

☑ Signatures of participants

Announce Your Plans

In addition to finding partners to help you take action, you might also find spectators. Publicize your plans and invite people from the community to observe, along with members of the media and local government. Put a spotlight on your act!

Get Social

Are you a fan of social media? Create an account for your project to spread the word. Social media can be a great way to let others know what you're doing, share your progress, and inspire them to get involved.

Use the Media

The media can help you spread the news of your plans for action. As you develop your knowledge and gather resources, keep tabs on any local reporters or bloggers who regularly cover water and environmental issues. Keep them posted as you make progress, and be sure to send a press release to every media outlet you can when the time for action arrives.

Inform Policy Makers

Invite local, regional, or state leaders and influential people to observe or take part in your event or action. Give them plenty of notice ahead of time and send reminders as the event date approaches. Keep track of who the best contact person is in their offices and keep them posted on developments. Influencing our policymakers secures our future!

Got Grants?

Can young people get grants or funds to turn their ideas into realities? Absolutely! Many organizations look for good ideas from teens who have the desire, the ability, and the resolve to champion a cause and change the world for the better. Where to start? Visit Youth Service America, a national organization that lists many of these opportunities, at ysa.org.

WRITING A PRESS RELEASE

The media want to know what you are planning and doing. If you have an event scheduled, alert the presses by creating a press release, which typically includes:

Of course you can add more details than this in your press release, and still be brief, clear, and enticing to make sure the press covers your event. Be sure to follow up with phone call or email reminders. You can also send press kits to the media that include more information about your organization or project.

Make Your Action Memorable

Get that camera poised to capture your success. Become a photo-journalist and documentarian to catch the story as it unfolds. Photographs and videos make great content for your project's social media accounts. Or perhaps you're a scrapbooker? If you like to cut and paste, save news articles, letters, photos of your activities, testimonials from friends who help out, and other pieces of your story and add them to the book.

Whether you choose to keep a journal, scrapbook, social media account, or website, remember to consistently capture the action all the way through so you can produce the visual story later. You may choose to include these visuals in a photomontage at a thank-you event with community partners, in an appreciation package that you send to funders, or in a proposal for your next action plan as proof that you can accomplish what you set out to do. Be sure to tell it like it is—record the frustrations (they are inevitable) along with the wins. This keeps the story authentic and serves as a helpful guide to others who may follow in your footsteps.

Remember: Your Actions Matter. Perhaps you were surprised or even amazed by some of the Teens in Action stories in this book. Every single person who has made change happen in this world started with an idea and a question: "Can I really do this?" They discovered the answer: "Yes." And if they can, *you* can too.

SUMMARY

Action. Action is perhaps the most important stage on your journey to help water, and you have made it count by investigating and preparing along the way. Whatever form your action takes—direct or indirect service, advocacy, or research—and whatever the results that occur, you have made your move toward going blue.

STAGE 4
THINK BACK→REFLECT

Do you sometimes press pause when watching a video or listening to a song to think about what you've just seen or heard? Reflection, the fourth stage on your water journey, is like that—it's a chance to pause and think about your experience from many angles, and also to learn from your slipups and successes.

The Story of Tar Creek: Part 4

Miami, Oklahoma, United States

How Did They Reflect?

"Have we made a change in the community?" Students considered the impact of their actions in various ways, always connecting their thoughts and feelings to the experience. Reflection happens through quiet moments, discussion, writing, photography, and providing feedback to others that improves the ongoing work. All voices are welcome, all are heard.

So after nearly four decades as a Superfund site, has the Tar Creek area changed? Unfortunately—not enough. Even with the federal, state, county, city, and tribal governments involved, as well as the Environmental Protection Agency, Centers for Disease Control and Prevention, and Harvard University . . . change is often very slow.

> **"** Children have enough problems in the world—they do not need this lurking behind them too. This is Mother Earth and we are supposed to take care of her and she will take care of us, but I think that we are severely slacking on our part.**"**
> —*Jessica Sage, Miami school student*

time for
REFLECTION

Dangerous waters can be found in many places. Toxic sites will only increase unless we clean up our act and work to restore these areas to their original abundance. Your generation stands to inherit this problem. Talk about this with a friend, teacher, or family member. Who should be responsible for these messes? What can be done now?

The Story of Tar Creek continues on page 138.

Pause, Look Back & Reflect

All through *Going Blue* you've encountered Time for Reflection boxes that encouraged you to hit the pause button and consider, contemplate, ponder, digest, look back, and r-e-f-l-e-c-t. It's a good habit to adopt in all parts of your life. Just as water reflects our images back to us and lets us consider ourselves from a different perspective, taking time to reflect on our lives and our world helps us become more considerate of the environment that depends on us.

"What are the best times to reflect on the course of your life? Whenever you are near water, such as the ocean, a quiet pond, or a small stream. Bodies of water help to stimulate your creative thought process."—Jeff Davidson, author of *Breathing Space*

HERE ARE SOME ADDITIONAL QUESTIONS TO HELP YOU FLEX YOUR REFLECTION MUSCLES.

- Of all the Teens in Action stories you read in this book, which one sticks in your head at this very moment? Why?

- Who is a likely partner for you in your plan to go blue? What will convince this person (or people) to get involved?

- Close your eyes and imagine our oceans and waterways restored and healthy. Picture sparkling blue water, swarms of colorful fish, vibrant coral reefs, pristine glacial lakes, clear deep rivers, and vast litter-free wetlands teeming with life. Which change would make you the most excited?

- How has learning about our oceans and waterways changed your daily habits or actions?

- What actions will you take to preserve and restore our waterways and keep this planet of ours healthy, dependable, and safe?

- Think of a person you want to influence to go blue. Write a passionate statement that sums up your message and come up with a memorable way to deliver your words (on a card shaped like a fish, perhaps?).

- Our water systems frequently face threats—from overfishing to oil spills. Think of a recent incident and compose your thoughts and feelings in a poem, song, rap, or comic strip. Then share with others.

- Imagine the year is 2050. Reflect on the changes you have seen on this water planet of ours. How were you part of the solution?

- Imagine that you are packing a suitcase for a trip, and you only have room for three words to take along that will be your reminders to go blue. Select with care. Pack them well. Share often.

- What have you discovered about yourself?

SUMMARY

Reflection. To get where you're going in helping the world's waters, you have to know where you've been. Through reflection, you build wisdom and ensure that every lesson and insight is valued on this journey. Reflection keeps you on track, reminds you to think through each important decision, and brings to light the golden opportunities presented to you to better yourself and your world.

STAGE 5
TELL IT→DEMONSTRATE

By now you have taken some action . . . from saving water in your own home, to cutting water use at school, fighting runoff pollution, picking up trash along a beach, or helping repopulate a river with fish. Now is the time to shout your story from the rooftops—and the water towers! During Demonstration, the fifth stage of going blue, you will inform the world what you did, how you did it, who was involved, what you learned, and what the results were.

The Story of Tar Creek: Part 5

Miami, Oklahoma, United States

How Did They Demonstrate?

Change at Tar Creek may be slow, yet the students remained persistent. They kept writing books and hosting conferences. According to Rebecca Jim, who now devotes all her time to this effort through the LEAD agency:

> Change is happening. It takes time and continued involvement of citizens, students, and in our case the states and the tribes. The government is people driven. Voices can be heard and in our case, young people's voices. If these voices stop, the government's efforts can be diverted, since it is driven by what these voices say.
>
> As the years have passed, the students who took on the Tar Creek challenge have become active members in their communities as parents of their own children. They have become professionals: dentists, teachers, attorneys, with several elected to public office and tribal leadership roles. And they are active in the environmental justice organization they inspired.

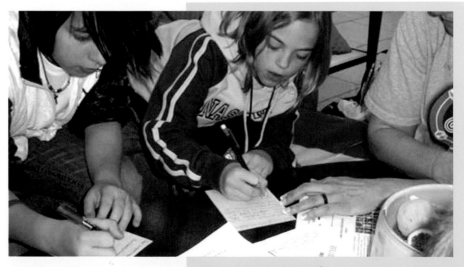

Miami students writing letters photo credit: Rebecca Jim

The World Awaits:
Tell Your Story

Here are some valuable tips on how to get in the papers (and on computer screens), inform the community, and keep your voice echoing loud and clear.

Be BOLD! Stand up and tell your story.

Know Your Audience. Who will you tell your story to? The media, a business, the school board, a parent organization, younger students, politicians, a college class—be sure to frame the story you tell for your particular audience.

Be Dynamic! Use all your creative energy to make your show-and-tell as lively as possible. Avoid the typical "This is what we did" spiel, and instead:

- Use drama (act out penguins in peril).
- Create a mock game show (quiz the audience about ocean acidification).
- Do a choral reading (quite unexpected).
- Create a short video that blends timelapse and hyperlapse video with key comments by participants.
- Stage a surprise entrance with an alarming report and challenge the group to come up with solutions.

Whatever you choose, engage your audience and challenge them to leave with at least one plan of action to improve our water environment. Review and use the Elevator Speech on page 119. It's a powerful tool!

Inform Policy Makers . . . *Again!* Did they show up when you did your action? If so, send them a huge THANKS! If they didn't show up, that's okay—send them photos, a video, or a collection of comments to show them how people got together in the community and took charge to make change. Then, perhaps next time you call for their attention, they'll answer.

Once You Know It— Show It!

With all this expertise, now is the time for you to take the mantle of leadership. You can proudly and boldly become a spokesperson for our oceans and waterways. Picture it: squads of cheerleading fish, dolphins, and jellies shouting, "Go, Team, Go!"

- Share what you know with others—kids and adults alike.

- Create a Going Blue club.

- Start a "Blue Blog."

- Write a comic book or graphic novel detailing your adventures.

- Chronicle your project on social media.

- Make a film or short video about your experience.

- Keep the adventure going.

- Become the eco-leader you were born to be.

SUMMARY

Demonstration. By demonstrating your service to others you've taken the crucial step to inform your community and the world about what can be done and what is *being* done to help save our oceans and waterways from distress. Demonstration will likely get others on board with you to help in future endeavors or guide them in going blue journeys of their own.

What's Next?

Congratulations! You have completed your own going blue adventure.
Of course, this is only the beginning. Next, you can (and probably *will*) find ways to stay active and continue to apply your passions, skills, talents, and knowledge to protect our world for generations to come. Now it's your turn to venture downstream or offshore, seek out more Earth-saving adventures, and produce even more spectacular results.

EarthEcho International's **Water Challenge** is a call-to-action that engages young people to protect and restore our water planet through service learning. Log onto monitorwater.org for tools and resources that you can use to stand up for a healthy future now. Joining the World Water Monitoring Challenge will help you go blue and stay blue!

Blue Books & Websites

You are definitely not floating alone out there. Check out these teen-friendly websites for ideas, information, and examples of what young people can do to go blue.

Websites

EarthEcho International (earthecho.org) is a nonprofit organization that empowers young people to take action to protect and restore our water planet. EarthEcho inspires kids and teens to make global change by meeting local needs, helping them to understand the connections between community priorities and current critical ocean and water-related issues. The organization was founded by siblings Philippe and Alexandra Cousteau in honor of their father Philippe Cousteau Sr., son of the legendary explorer Jacques Cousteau.

4ocean (4ocean.com) is an organization dedicated to cleaning up trash from the ocean and coastlines, one pound at a time.

H2O for Life (h2oforlifeschools.org) provides curriculum for schools to study the issues surrounding water in local communities as well as the global water crisis. Students learn how to be stewards of the earth while taking action to bring water, sanitation, and hygiene education to a global partner school in need.

Ocean Conservancy (oceanconservancy.org) promotes healthy and diverse ocean ecosystems and opposes practices that threaten oceanic and human life. Its members advocate real leadership with cooperation among governments, businesses, scientists, policymakers, conservation organizations, and citizen activists. Together, they aim to create concrete solutions that lead to lasting change, so our oceans can be experienced for generations to come.

Your Environment, Your Choice (epa.gov/students) is a website provided by the United States' Environmental Protection Agency that invites teens to think, act, and find helpful resources regarding issues in the environment. Includes information about environmental careers.

Books

50 Ways to Save the Ocean by David Helvarg (Inner Ocean Publishing, 2006). This well-researched book explores simple, everyday actions that protect and restore the ocean, from recycling plastic to buying locally grown produce. It also addresses issues of runoff pollution, wetland destruction, coral reef damage, and overfishing. Foreword by Philippe Cousteau.

A Bigger Picture: My Fight to Bring a New African Voice to the Climate Crisis by Vanessa Nakate (Mariner Books, 2021). Activist Vanessa Nakate went from college student to global climate leader. Follow her story of the disproportionate effects of climate change on the African continent and her home country, Uganda. Vanessa describes how race, gender, and geography intersect to leave the least responsible for climate change with the biggest problems.

> **"** Three of my favorite books that address sustainability issues are *50 Ways to Save the Ocean* by David Helvarg, *Cradle to Cradle* by William McDonough and Michael Braungart, and the mother of all environmental books *Silent Spring* by Rachel Carson. **"**
> —Philippe Cousteau

Coral Reefs: Cities of the Ocean by Maris Wicks (First Second, 2016). "We need to protect biodiversity to maintain food sources, symbioses, habitat, and so on." This nonfiction comic is filled with colorful images, amazing facts (did you know coral is an animal?), info on biodiversity, underwater creatures, and challenges we face today.

Cradle to Cradle: Remaking the Way We Make Things by William McDonough and Michael Braungart (North Point Press, 2002). According to the authors of this book, most environmental pollution is the result of poor product design. Products can instead be designed to serve their function and, once discarded, to actually nourish the environment or provide high-quality materials for technical production. A manifesto of "eco-effectiveness."

The First Rule of Climate Club by Carrie Firestone (G.P. Putnam's Sons, 2022). In this novel, eighth grader Mary Kate Murphy and other climate-aware teens join a class to take action. Food waste, idling cars, fast fashion, and composting become priorities along with social justice inequities. With persistence and determination, and in spite of an ineffective mayor, the Climate Club makes big impact! A blueprint for action.

Oceans for Dummies by Ashlan Cousteau and Philippe Cousteau, with Joe Kraynak (John Wiley & Sons, 2021). Literally everything you could want to know about oceans is presented in this book with compelling narratives, memorable images, and facts galore. Truly an adventure into our planet's most exciting frontier: our ocean!

Silent Spring by Rachel Carson (Mariner Books, 2002). First published in 1962, this landmark book alerted a large audience to the environmental and human dangers of careless use of pesticides, spurring revolutionary changes in the laws affecting our air, land, and water.

Two Degrees by Alan Gratz (Scholastic, 2022). In this novel, teens confront high jeopardy in California when drought causes deadly wildfires, in the Canadian tundra as polar bears migrate to town due to climate change, and in Miami when a big hurricane hits. Our urgent climate crises ultimately bring these youth together to tell their stories and take action.

We Are All Greta: Be Inspired by Greta Thunberg to Save the World by Valentina Giannella (Laurence King, 2019). "Humans are very adaptable: We can still fix this. But the opportunity to do so will not last for long. We must start today. We have no more excuses." These words are from climate activist Greta Thunberg. Follow her pathway to activism that has aims to change policy to protect our planet.

Sources for Blue Facts

What Do You Know?
The Canadian Press. "Human Overfishing Starves Dolphins, Sharks, Seabirds: Study." *The Canadian Press*. March 2, 2009.

National Oceanic and Atmospheric Administration. "State of the Climate Global Analysis 2009." National Climatic Data Center, United States Department of Commerce.

STAGE 1: Find Out→Investigate
The Story of Tar Creek: Parts #1–5
LEAD Agency, Inc. "Facts." (leadagency.org)

United States Census Bureau, American Community Survey. Population data, 2015–2018.

United States Environmental Protection Agency, Office of Land and Emergency Management, 2020. Data collected includes: Superfund site information from SEMS as of the end of FY2019 and site boundary data from FY2014 FOIA Request.

You're All Wet!
Alter, Alexandra. "Yet Another 'Footprint' to Worry About: Water: Taking a Cue from Carbon Tracking, Companies and Conservationists Tally Hidden Sources of Consumption." *The Wall Street Journal*. February 17, 2009.

The American Water Works Association (AWWA). "55 Facts, Figures & Follies of Water Conservation." Denver Water Department, Denver, CO. 2001.

Human Development Report Office. "Human Development Report 2006: Beyond Scarcity: Power, Poverty and the Global Water Crisis." United Nations Development Programme.

Leal, Fermin. "Sonora High School's 'Water Guardians' Inspire Proposed Conservation Law." OCDE Newsroom, April 21, 2017. (newsroom.ocde.us/sonora-high-schools-water-guardians-inspire-proposed-conservation-law)

NYC Environmental Protection. "Water Use Calculation." (nyc.gov/assets/dep/downloads/pdf/environment/education/sewers-activity-water-use-calculation.pdf)

Statistica. (statistica.com)

US Geological Society Water Science School. "Water Q & A: How Much Water Do I Use at Home Each Day?" (usgs.gov/special-topics/water-science-school/science/water-qa-how-much-water-do-i-use-home-each-day)

Washington Suburban Sanitary Commission. "Water Usage Chart."

Water Footprint Network. (waterfootprint.org)

Water Footprint Network. "Water Footprint Product Gallery." (waterfootprint.org/en/resources/interactive-tools/product-gallery/)

Water, Water, Everywhere . . . or Is It?
The MarineBio Conservation Society. "Did You Know...? Marine Life/Ocean Facts." (marinebio.org/creatures/facts/)

National Marine Sanctuaries. "Education." (sanctuaries.noaa.gov/education)

Save the Sea. "Interesting Ocean Facts." (savethesea.org/STS%20ocean_facts.htm)

Community Water Needs
Potable Water
Felton, Ryan, Lisa Gill, and Lewis Kendall. "We Sampled Tap Water Across the US—and Found Arsenic, Lead, and Toxic Chemicals." *The Guardian*. March 31, 2021. (theguardian.com/us-news/2021/mar/31/americas-tap-water-samples-forever-chemicals)

Human Development Report Office. "Human Development Report 2006: Beyond Scarcity: Power, Poverty and the Global Water Crisis." United Nations Development Programme. (hdr.undp.org/content/human-development-report-2006)

Mundra, Raj. "Does Community Service Really Change Anything: Our Group of Teens Discovered the Answer Is Complex." *The Christian Science Monitor*. December 29, 2008.

A Thirsty World in Crisis
Copeny, Mari. (maricopeny.com)

Flint Rising. (flintrising.com)

Good Morning America. "5 Years into Water Crisis, Little Miss Flint Hasn't Given Up | GMA." April 22, 2019. (youtu.be/7tvm8A0J3lg)

Mahoney, Adam. "Eight Years Later, Flint's Water Crisis Rages On." Capital B. May 25, 2022. (capitalbnews.org/flint-michigan-epa-audit-lead-water-crisis/)

NowThis News. "Flint Water Crisis' Little Miss Flint Mari Copeny Hosts Fundraiser for Bottled Water | NowThis." April 26, 2018. (youtu.be/3Qnk7Ou4yLQ)

World Health Organization. "Drinking-Water." Updated March 21, 2022. (who.int/news-room/fact-sheets/detail/drinking-water)

Water Privatization
The Carter Center. (cartercenter.org)

Center for the Study of Social Change, Institutions and Policy (SCIP). Schar School of Public Policy, George Mason University. (scip.gmu.edu)

FLOW: How Did a Handful of Corporations Steal Our Water? "About Water."

Global Policy Forum. "Water in Conflict." (archive.globalpolicy.org/security-council/dark-side-of-natural-resources/water-in-conflict.html)

Royte, Elizabeth. *Bottlemania: Big Business, Local Springs, and the Battle Over America's Drinking Water*. New York: Bloomsbury Publishing, 2009.

Water.org. "The Water Crisis." (water.org/our-impact/water-crisis/)

Whiteley, John M., Helen Ingram, and Richard Warren Perry, eds. *Water, Place, & Equity*. Cambridge: Massachusetts Institute of Technology, 2008.

Bottled Water
AllAboutWater.org. "The Effects of Bottled Water on the Environment."

Clark Howard, Brian. "Message in a Bottle: Despite the Hype, Bottled Water Is Neither CLEANER nor GREENER Than Tap Water." *E: The Environmental Magazine* 14, no. 5 (September/October 2003).

The Container Recycling Institute. "Bottled Water." (container-recycling.org/index.php/issues/bottled-water)

Grand View Research. *Reusable Water Bottle Market Size, Share & Trends Analysis Report by Material Type (Glass, Plastic, Stainless Steel), by Distribution Channel (Supermarkets & Hypermarkets, Online), by Region, and Segment Forecasts, 2022–2030.* grandviewresearch.com/industry-analysis/reusable-water-bottle-market.

Hoffman, Sue. "Students Tap into Bottle-Waste Stream." *Chagrin Valley Times*. April 29, 2009.

Senate Hearing 110-1264. *Quality and Environmental Impacts of Bottled Water. Hearing before the Subcommittee on Transportation Safety, Infrastructure Security, and Water Quality of the Committee on Environment and Public Works*. United States Senate, 110th Congress, Second Session. September 10, 2008. (govinfo.gov/content/pkg/CHRG-110shrg88908/html/CHRG-110shrg88908.htm)

Tappening. "Why Not Bottled Water?"

Where's the Water in Your Backyard?
United States Environmental Protection Agency. "What Is a Watershed?"

Your Piece of the Watershed
Rivers and Creeks
American Rivers. *America's Most Endangered Rivers: 2021 Edition*. Washington, DC: Author, 2021.

United States Environmental Protection Agency, Office of Water. *EPA's Beach Report: 2018 Swimming Season*. July 2019. (epa.gov/sites/default/files/2019-07/documents/beach-swimming-season-report-2018.pdf)

Wong, C.M., J. Pittock, U. Collier, and P. Schelle. *World's Top 10 Rivers at Risk*. Gland, Switzerland: World Wild Life International, March 2007.

Estuaries
Hoyle, Brian. "Bioaccumulation." JRank.org. (science.jrank.org/pages/854/Bioaccumulation.html)

Laffoley, Dan, and Gabriel Grimsditch, eds. *The Management of Natural Coastal Carbon Sinks*. Gland, Switzerland: International Union for Conservation of Nature and Natural Resources, 2009.

Mr. Trash Wheel®. (mrtrashwheel.com)

Office of Naval Research: Science & Technology Focus. "Oceanography." "Habitats."

Lakes
Dorfman, Mark, and Kirsten Sinclair Rosselot. *Testing the Waters: A Guide to Water Quality at Vacation Beaches.* New York: The Natural Resources Defense Council, 2009.

Ishii, Satoshi, Dennis L. Hansen, Randall E. Hicks, and Michael J. Sadowsky. "Beach Sand and Sediments Are Temporal Sinks and Sources of *Escherichia coli* in Lake Superior." *Environmental Science & Technology* 41 no. 7 (2007): 2203–2209.

Coastal Areas
Diaz, Robert J., and Rutger Rosenberg. "Spreading Dead Zones and Consequences for Marine Ecosystems." *Science* 321 (2008): 926–929.

Howard, Jenny. "Dead Zones, Explained." *National Geographic.* July 31, 2019. (nationalgeographic.com/environment/article/dead-zones)

Muth, David. "Ten Years After the BP Oil Spill, Restoration Offers Hope for the Gulf." National Wildlife Federation, June 8, 2020. (blog.nwf.org/2020/04/ten-years-after-the-bp-oil-spill-restoration-offers-hope-for-the-gulf)

National Geographic. "Dead Zone." (education.nationalgeographic.org/resource/dead-zone)

Office of Naval Research: Science & Technology Focus. "Oceanography" "Habitats."

STAGE 2: Dive In→Prepare
The Amazing Ocean
National Marine Sanctuaries. "Education." (sanctuaries.noaa.gov/education)

National Oceanic and Atmospheric Administration. "Ocean." United States Department of Commerce. (noaa.gov/ocean.html)

The Carbon Conundrum: Part #1—Ocean Acidification
The Natural Resources Defense Council. "Ocean Acidification: What You Need to Know." (nrdc.org/stories/what-you-need-know-about-ocean-acidification)

Sabine, Christopher L., Richard A. Feely, Nicolas Gruber, Robert M. Key, Kitack Lee, John L. Bullister, Rik Wanninkhof, et. al. "The Oceanic Sink for Anthropogenic CO2." *Science* 305 (2004): 367–371.

Food Chain, Interrupted
McKie, Robin. "Arctic Seas Turn to Acid, Putting Vital Food Chain at Risk." *The Guardian*, October 4, 2009. (theguardian.com/world/2009/oct/04/arctic-seas-turn-to-acid)

Sample, Ian. "Unexpected Rise in Carbon-Fuelled Ocean Acidity Threatens Shellfish, Say Scientists." *The Guardian*. November 25, 2008. (theguardian.com/environment/2008/nov/25/water-ocean-acidity-shellfish)

The Carbon Conundrum: Part #2—Climate Change
Gagosian, Robert B. *Abrupt Climate Change: Should We Be Worried?* Woods Hole, MA: The Woods Hole Oceanographic Institution, 2003.

The Global Conveyor Belt
National Ocean Service. "The Global Conveyor Belt." National Oceanic and Atmospheric Administration, United States Department of Commerce.

"I'm Melting!"
Hu, Aixue, Gerald Meehl, Weiqing Han, and Jianjun Yin. "Transient Response of the MOC and Climate to Potential Melting of the Greenland Ice Sheet in the 21st Century." *Geophysical Research Letters*. May 27, 2009.

Marian Koshland Science Museum of the National Academy of Sciences. "Amplifiers: Ice-Reflectivity Feedback."

Myers, Steven Lee, Andrew C. Revkin, Simon Romero, and Clifford Krauss. "Old Ways of Life Are Fading as the Arctic Thaws." *The New York Times*. October 20, 2005.

Windows to the Universe. "The Cryosphere and Global Climate Change." University Corporation for Atmospheric Research. (windows2universe.org/earth/polar/cryosphere_climate1.html)

Windows to the Universe. "Warming of the Polar Regions." University Corporation for Atmospheric Research. (windows2universe.org/earth/polar/polar_climate.html)

Plastics, Pollution & Trash
Greenpeace. "Protect the Oceans." (greenpeace.org/usa/campaigns/oceans)

Ocean Conservancy. (oceanconservancy.org)

Ocean Conservancy. "We Clean On: International Coastal Cleanup 2021 Report." (oceanconservancy.org/wp-content/uploads/2021/09/2020-ICC-Report_Web_FINAL-0909.pdf)

The Great Pacific Garbage Patch
Basu, Saikat. "The Largest 'Landfill' on Earth; the Great Pacific Garbage Patch." *Digital Journal*. July 28, 2008.

Biodegradable Products Institute. "The Compostable Logo." (www.bpiworld.org/BPI-Public/Program.html)

Bonfiglio, Jon. "Humans Eating Plastic—Over 40 Pounds in a Lifetime." Plastic Oceans. December 15, 2020. (plasticoceans.org/humans-eating-plastic-over-40-pounds-in-a-lifetime/)

Cava, Marco R. "Birds, Boats Threatened by Great Garbage Patch." *USA Today*. November 16, 2009, Life Section.

Ferreira, Fionn. (fionnferreira.com)

Greenberg, Paul. "The Oceans' Junkyards (a review of *Flotsametrics and the Floating World: How One Man's Obsession with Runaway Sneakers and Rubber Ducks Revolutionized Ocean Science* by Curtis Ebbesmeyer and Eric Scigliano). *The New York Times Book Review*. May 14, 2009.

McNally, Shelagh. "Searching for a 'Green Plastic' Solution," *Financial Post* (Canada). May 29, 2009.

The Ocean Cleanup. "Founder and CEO Boyan Slat." (theoceancleanup.com/boyan-slat)

Plastic Oceans. (plasticoceans.org)

Runoff Pollution
National Oceanic and Atmospheric Administration. "International Year of the Ocean—Kids' & Teachers' Resources."

Coral Reefs in Crisis
Fitzgerald, Sunny. "The Super-Corals of the Red Sea."
BBC Future Planet, April 8, 2020. (bbc.com/future/article/20200408-the-middle-eastern-corals-that-could survive-climate-change)

Gibbens, Sarah. "Climate-Resilient Coral Species Offer Hope for the World's Reefs." National Geographic, March 10, 2022. (nationalgeographic.com/environment/article/climate-resilient-coral species-offer-hope-for-world-reefs)

National Science Foundation. "Some Coral Reefs Are Keeping Pace with Ocean Warming." September 13, 2021. (beta.nsf.gov/news/some-coral-reefs-are-keeping-pace-ocean-warming)

Office of Naval Research: Science & Technology Focus. "Oceanography." "Habitats."

Looking Back: Historical Moments & Actions
A Brief History of Ocean Exploration
Hrbek, Ivan. "Ibn Battuta: Muslim Explorer and Writer." *Encyclopedia Britannica*. Accessed September 18, 2022. (britannica.com/biography/Ibn-Battuta)

Lo, Jung-pang. "Zheng He: Chinese Admiral and Diplomat." *Encyclopedia Britannica*. Updated September 12, 2022. (britannica.com/biography/Zheng-He)

McLaughlin, Charles H., Jr. "Our Blue Planet: Ocean Exploration." *Technology and Children*. December 1, 2005.

Animal Lifeguards: Eugenia Clark & Archie Carr
Ehrenfeld, David. M.D. "Archie Carr Tribute." Sea Turtle Conservancy. (conserveturtles.org/about-stc-archie-carr-tribute/)

MISS (Minorities in Shark Sciences). (misselasmo.org)

"Shark Scientist Jasmin Graham on the Importance of Diversifying Marine Conservation." *World Wildlife Magazine*. Fall 2022.

STAGE 3: Get Going→Act!
Your Little Choices Make a Big Splash
The Conscious Club. "Water & Clothing." May 15, 2019. (theconsciouschallenge. org/ecologicalfootprintbibleoverview/water-clothing)

Earth 911. "E-waste: Harmful Materials." (earth911.com/electronics/ e-waste-harmful-materials)

United States Environmental Protection Agency. "Pollution Prevention (P2) Education Toolbox: Tools for Helping Teachers Integrate P2 Concepts in the Classroom." EPA-905-F-97-011. August 1997.

Farming & Food
Marks, Susan J. *Aqua Shock: The Water Crisis in America*. New York: Bloomburg Press, 2009.

Overfishing
Greenpeace. "Protect the Oceans." (greenpeace.org/usa/campaigns/oceans)

Planet Tuna. "Atlantic Bluefin Tuna: The Path to an Amazing Recovery." (planet tuna.com/en/atlantic-bluefin-tuna-the-path-to-an-amazing-recovery/)

Roach, John. "Seafood May Be Gone by 2048, Study Says." *National Geographic*. November 2, 2006.

Take Action
Greenpeace. (greenpeace.org)

Ocean Conservancy. (oceanconservancy.org)

National Oceanic and Atmospheric Administration. United States Department of Commerce. (noaa.gov)

United States Environmental Protection Agency. (epa.gov)

INDEX

Additional Photo Credits

Cover, (coral reef) © Andrey Kuzmin | iStock.com; (turtle) © Colin Davis | iStock.com • **Contents,** © Folyflex | Dreamstime.com; © Georgette Douwma • **Page vii** (listed top to bottom), © BananaStock; © BananaStock; © Stockbyte; © Nasser Buhamad | Dreamstime.com • **Page 1** (listed top to bottom), © BananaStock; © BananaStock; © Stockbyte • **Pages 8–9,** © Vladvitek | Dreamstime.com • **Page 9,** © Stephen Finn | Dreamstime.com • **Page 11,** © Pineapple Studio | istockphoto.com • **Pages 16–17,** © istockphoto.com/PhilAugustavo • **Page 20** (listed top to bottom), © istockphoto.com/xua; © istockphoto.com/CostinT; © istockphoto.com/alexsl; © istockphoto.com/Vermette; © istockphoto.com/Greywind; © istockphoto.com/Aeolos • **Page 22,** © Marzanna Syncerz | Dreamstime.com • **Page 23** (listed top to bottom), © Marcello Renda | Dreamstime.com; © Zoommer | Dreamstime.com; © PhotoDisc; © PhotoDisc; © istockphoto.com/travismanley, © istockphoto.com/stuartbur; © PhotoDisc; © istockphoto.com/kcline; (red mug) © Lgrig | Dreamstime.com; © Scanrail | istockphoto.com • **Page 27,** © Nikolai Sorokin | Dreamstime.com • **Pages 28–29,** © NASA image by Robert Simmon and Reto Stöckli • **Page 34,** © Kevin Brown | Dreamstime.com • **Page 37,** © Dmitry Naumov | Dreamstime.com • **Page 38,** © Bidouze Stéphane | Dreamstime.com • **Page 40,** © EasternLightcraft | istockphoto.com • **Page 43,** © John Wollwerth | Dreamstime.com • **Page 46,** © Kevin Keen | istockphoto.com • **Page 49,** © Tim Pleasant | Dreamstime.com • **Page 51,** © Peter Wollinga | Shutterstock • **Pages 56–57,** © Andre Nantel | Dreamstime.com • **Page 61,** © Yuri Arcurs | Dreamstime.com • **Pages 62–63,** (penguins and iceberg) © Martin Fischer | Dreamstime.com; (ocean surface) © Rgbspace | Dreamstime.com; (fishing boats) © Kmitu | Dreamstime.com; (freight ship) © Aleksey Bakaleev | Dreamstime.com; (San Fransisco coast) © Blain Thomas | Dreamstime.com; (shark) © Andrejs Pidjass | Dreamstime.com; (seal lions) © Moswyn | Dreamstime.com; (school of fish) © Piboon Srimak | Dreamstime.com; (water below surface) © Addict | Dreamstime.com; (coral reef) © Stephankerkhofs | Dreamstime.com; (yellow fish) © Michael Shake | Dreamstime.com • **Page 67,** © FernandoQuevedo | istockphoto.com • **Page 70,** © Jan Martin Will | Dreamstime.com • **Page 71,** © NASA image by Jeff Schmaltz (visibleearth.nasa.gov) • **Page 79,** © Placebo365 | istockphoto.com • **Page 82,** © istockphoto.com/ EricFerguson • **Page 85,** (top) © dreamstime.com; (bottom) © Tasha Kenyon • **Page 91,** © istockphoto.com/PacoRomero • **Page 99,** © Luciano Mortula | Dreamstime.com • **Page 104,** © IvanSpasic | istockphoto.com • **Pages 106–107,** © Greg Epperson | Dreamstime.com • **Page 112,** © Wally Stemberger | Dreamstime.com • **Pages 116–117,** © Michael Zysman | Dreamstime.com • **Page 123,** © Argusimages | Dreamstime.com • **Page 129** (listed left to right, top to bottom), Local residents monitor the the daily fish catch in Andavadoaka, Madagascar. Photo credit: Anne Furr/Marine Photobank; A duck is cleaned by volunteers after Norway's catastrophic oil spill, 2009. Photo credit: Linda Schonknecht/Marine Photobank; Coral Cay Conservation workers cleaning a beach in the Philippines. Photo credit: Howard Peters 2008/Marine Photobank; Community cleanup at the municipal dumpsite in Patagonia, Chile. Photo credit: Tom Crowley/Marine Photobank. • **Pages 130–131,** © Marek Uliasz | Dreamstime.com • **Page 133,** © Tomas1111 | Dreamstime.com • **Page 134,** © Eric Isselée | Dreamstime.com • **Pages 136–137,** © James Hardy/PhotoAlto/Corbis • **Page 139,** © Clearviewstock | Dreamstime.com • **Pages 140–141,** © Nicemonkey | Dreamstime.com • **Page 142,** © Tommy Schultz | Dreamstime.com

About the Authors

Cathryn Berger Kaye, M.A., is an international education consultant and former classroom teacher. She promotes youth being effective changemakers at conferences around the world and works with students, teachers, schools, and organizations. Cathy's books include *Make a Splash! A Kid's Guide to Protecting Earth's Ocean, Lakes, Rivers & Wetlands* (with Philippe Cousteau), *The Complete Guide to Service Learning*, and the How to Take Action! series of student workbooks. While Cathy enjoys traveling, she is glad to feel the ocean breezes at her home in Los Angeles. Most of all, she adores her family—husband, Barry, two daughters, Ariel and Devora, and grandchildren—who inspire her daily.

Philippe Cousteau is an Emmy-nominated filmmaker and TV host, ocean explorer, social entrepreneur, and environmental advocate. He is the grandson of the legendary Jacques Cousteau—the man who invented scuba diving and introduced the world to life under the sea. He is the founder of EarthEcho International, a leading nonprofit organization creating a global youth movement to protect and restore our ocean. He has authored numerous books, hosted television shows for the BBC, Discovery Channel, Travel Channel, CNN, and more. He lives in Los Angeles with his wife, Ashlan, two daughters, rescue dog, and two chickens.

Email the authors at help4kids@freespirit.com.

Teachers and other adults: Download the free online Leader's Guide at freespirit.com/leader.